A NAME FOR YOUR BABY

PENGUIN BOOKS

PENGUIN BOOKS
Published by the Penguin Group
Penguin Group (NZ), 67 Apollo Drive, Mairangi Bay,
Auckland 1310, New Zealand (a division of Pearson New Zealand Ltd)
Penguin Group (USA) Inc., 375 Hudson Street,
New York, New York 10014, USA
Penguin Group (Canada), 90 Eglinton Avenue East, Suite 700, Toronto,
Ontario, M4P 2Y3, Canada (a division of Pearson Penguin Canada Inc.)
Penguin Books Ltd, 80 Strand, London, WC2R 0RL, England
Penguin Ireland, 25 St Stephen's Green,
Dublin 2, Ireland (a division of Penguin Books Ltd)
Penguin Group (Australia), 250 Camberwell Road, Camberwell,
Victoria 3124, Australia (a division of Pearson Australia Group Pty Ltd)
Penguin Books India Pvt Ltd, 11, Community Centre,
Panchsheel Park, New Delhi - 110 017, India
Penguin Books (South Africa) (Pty) Ltd, 24 Sturdee Avenue,
Rosebank, Johannesburg 2196, South Africa

Penguin Books Ltd, Registered Offices: 80 Strand, London, WC2R 0RL, England

First published by Penguin Group (NZ), 2006
1 3 5 7 9 10 8 6 4 2

Copyright © Penguin Group (NZ) 2006

The right of Penguin Group (NZ) to be identified as the author of this work in terms of
section 96 of the Copyright Act 1994 is hereby asserted.

Designed by Mary Egan
Typeset by Egan Reid Ltd
Printed in Australia by McPherson's Printing Group

ISBN 13: 978 0 14 3005971
ISBN 10: 0 14 300597 9
A catalogue record for this book is available
from the National Library of New Zealand.

www.penguin.co.nz

Introduction

When choosing a name for your baby there are several points that should be considered.

First of all, the name must go well with your surname. Compare the lengths of the surname and the Christian names – will the complete name take half an hour to say or is it nicely balanced? Make sure that the name isn't a tongue twister – the sounds should blend and flow smoothly.

Remember to check the initials to make sure that they don't spell out some comic or unfortunate word. Likely shortened forms must also be considered.

Look at the meaning and origin of the name. If your choice is rather exotic, you could consider making it a second name, particularly if it is difficult to spell or pronounce.

Names are affected by changing tastes and fashions, so consider how quickly a name is likely to date, and whether a very cute, popular name for a little boy will seem equally convincing for a grown man.

This selection includes names from a variety of languages and most names are given with their origin and meaning, as well as some alternative meanings, variant spellings, or shortened forms.

Abbreviations

A	Arabic	L	Latin
Af	African	M	Maori
Au	Australian	N	Norse
C	Celtic	NA	North American Indian
Ch	Chinese	OE	Old English
E	English	P	Persian
F	French	R	Russian
Ga	Gaelic	S	Spanish
Gk	Greek	Sa	Sanskrit
H	Hebrew	Sc	Scandinavian
Ha	Hawaiian	Sl	Slavic
I	Italian	T	Teutonic
Ir	Irish	W	Welsh

Girls

Aba (A) born on a Thursday
Abella (H) beautiful one, breath
Abeni (A) prayed for
Abia (A) great
Abigail (H) father's joy. Abbey Abbie Abby Gail Gale Gayle
Abira (H) strong
Abra (H) mother of multitudes
Abril (L) month of April
Acacia (Gk) acacia flower. Cacia Casey
Acantha (Gk) prickly
Ada (T) joyful
Adah (H) ornament
Adalia (H) God will care for me. Adalie

Adaline (F) noble. Adeline
Adama (H) from the red earth. Adamina Adana Adanna
Adara (Gk) beautiful, virginal
Adela (T) noble. Adele Adelle Della
Adelaide (T) of noble birth. Ada Addy Adelia
Adelie (E) noble. Adelicia
Adelpha (Gk) sister. Adelfa
Adena (H) voluptuous. Adina
Adin (H) beautifully adorned one
Adiva (A) kind, gentle
Adoncia (S) sweet one
Adonia (Gk) goddess. Adona
Adora (L) beloved. Adoree Dora
Adriana (L) dark one. Adira Adriane Adrianna Adrianne Adrienne Hadria Hadriane
Adrienne see **Adriana**

5

Adromeda (Gk) ruler of men
Adya (Sa) ancient wise one. Adia
Africa (C) pleasant. Afrika
Agalia (Gk) joy
Agape (Gk) love
Agate (F) name of a precious stone
Agatha (Gk) good. Aggie
Agnes (Gk) pure. Aggie Akinehi Annis Ina Ines Inez Nessa Nessie Nest Nesta
Ahava (H) beloved
Aida (T) wise, rich, happy
Aidan (Ir) fiery one. Aideen Edana
Aiesha (A) woman
Aileen Irish form of **Evelyn**
Ailish (H) given to God
Ailsa (Af) life
Aimee French form of **Amy**
Aine (Ir) delight, joy
Ainsley (Ga) from one's own meadow. Ainslie Ansley
Airlie (Gk) ethereal
Aisha (Af) life
Aisiling (Ir) dream, vision. Aishinn Aislin
Aissa (Af) grateful
Akilina (L) one who soars
Akinehi Maori form of **Agnes**

Akira (H) to protect
Alaina see **Elaine**
Alameda (S) from the grove of cotton
Alana (Ga) fair child. Alanna Alina Lana
Alanis usage derived from US singer
Alavda (F) lark, the bird
Alba (I) fair one. Albany Albina Albinia Alvina
Alberta (T) bright, noble. Albertine Berta
Alcina (Gk) clever
Alda (T) old
Aldonza (S) sweet one
Aldora (E) noble
Alea (A) exalted. Aleah Alia Aliyah
Aleema (A) scholarly. Alema Alima
Alegria (S) happy, joyful
Alesa see **Alexandra**
Aleta (L) bird-like. Alouetta
Alethea (Gk) truth. Alethia
Alexandra (Gk) defender of man. Alesa Alessandra Alexa Alexandria Alexandrina Sacha Sandra Sandy Sasha Shandra Zandra

Alfreda (T) wise counsellor
Alice (Gk) truth. Ali Alicia
  Aline Alison Allison Ally
  Alyson Arihana
Alida (L) small, winged one.
  Aleda Aleta Aletta Alette
  Alidia Lida
Alima (A) musical
Alina (Sl) fair one. Alene
  Alyna
Alison Scottish form of **Alice**
Aliyyah (A) exalted. Aliya
Aliza (H) joyful. Aleeza Alizah
Allegra (L) cheerful
Allira (Au) quartz
Alma (L) loving
Almeta (L) ambitious.
  Almeda
Almira (A) exalted
Alodie (E) wealthy
Alpha (Gk) first, first born
Althea (Gk) healer. Thea
Alva (L) beautiful
Alvina (T) noble friend. Vina
Alvita (L) annointed
Alyssa (Gk) sane one
Ama (Af) born on Saturday
Amabel (L) lovable.
  Amabelle Amy Belle Mabel
  Mabelle

Amadora (I) gift of love.
  Amada
Amal (A) hopeful. Amala
  Amalia
Aman (Af) trustworthy,
  faithful
Amanda (L) fit to be loved.
  Manda Mandy
Amandala (Af) power
Amara (Gk) forever beautiful
Amaranth (Gk) everlasting
  flower. Amaranta
  Amarante
Amaris (E) child of the moon
Amaryllis (L) country girl
Amber (A) yellow jewel
Amberlee combination of
  Amber and **Lee**
Ambrosine (Gk) divine one.
  Ambrosia Ambrosina
Amelia (T) industrious.
  Amalia Amalie Ameline
  Emeline Emmeline Mellie
  Millie
Amethyst (Gk) the colour of
  wine
Amilee combination of **Amy**
  and **Lee**
Amina (A) honest
Aminta (Gr) protector

7

Amira (A) princess. Ameera
  Amirah
Amissa (H) friend
Amity (L) friendship
Amma (Sa) God-like
Amorita (S) beloved.
  Amorette
Amorosa (I) loved one.
  Amory
Amrita (Sa) immortal
Amy (F) beloved. Aimee
An (Ch) peace
Anais (F) fruitful
Anala (Sa) fiery one
Ananda (Sa) blissful
Anastasia (Gr) resurrection.
  Anastasie Anstice Stacey
  Stacie Stacy
Anatola (Gk) from the east
Anchoret (W) beloved
Andrea (L) womanly.
  Andreana Andree
Anela (Ha) angel
Anemone (Gk) frail flower
Angela (Gk) heavenly
  messenger. Angel Angele
  Angelina Angeline Angie
Angelica (L) angelic.
  Angelika Angelique
Angerin (F) angel of wine

Angharad (W) much loved.
  Anchoret
Ani Maori form of **Ann**
Anisa (A) tender. Aneesa
Anita (H) grace. Anitra
Ann (H) God has favoured
  me. Ani Anna Anne
  Annetta Annette Annie
  Anya Hanna Hannah Nan
  Nancy Nanette Nina
Anna see **Ann**
Annabelle (L) graceful,
  beautiful. Anabel Annabel
  Annabella
Annalisa combination of
  Anna and **Lisa**
Annamaria combination of
  Anna and **Maria**
Anne see **Ann**
Annelise combination of
  Anne and **Lise**. Annalies
  Annaliese Annelies
  Anneliese
Anona (L) fruitful
Anora (OE) light, graceful
Anouk (F) grace
Anthea (Gk) lady of flowers.
  Thea
Antonia (L) priceless.
  Anthonia Antoinette Toni
Aperira Maori from of **April**

Aphra (H) female deer
April (L) from the name of the month. Aperira
Ara (Gk) spirit of revenge
Arabel (L) beautiful altar. Arabella Arabelle
Araminta combination of **Arabel** and **Aminta**
Arcelia (S) treasure
Arddun (W) beautiful
Ardelia (L) zealous. Ardelis
Arden (OE) from the valley of the eagle
Aretha (Gk) best. Areta
Arethusa (Gk) virtuous
Aria (L) beautiful melody
Ariadne (Gk) very holy. Ariane Arianna
Ariel (H) lioness of God
Arihana Maori form of **Alison**
Arista (Gk) beautiful. Arissa
Arizona from the name of the US State
Arlene (Ga) pledge. Arlena
Armida (P) beautiful
Arnett (E) little eagle
Aroha (M) sympathy, understanding, love
Artemis (Gk) moon goddess. Artemisia

Artha (Sa) wealthy
Artia female form of Art, Arthur
Arwen (W) muse
Asenath (Af) belonging to the god Neith
Asenka (H) graceful
Asha (P) truth
Ashleigh (OE) of the ash tree. Ashley
Ashling (Ir) dream, vision
Asis (Af) sun
Aspasia (Gk) welcome
Aster (Gk) starry. Asta Astera Astra
Astrid (N) divine
Atalanta (Gk) mighty adversary. Atlanta
Athalie (H) God is mighty. Athalia
Athena (Gk) wisdom
Audrey (OE) noble strength. Audrie
Augusta (L) venerable. Auguste Augustina Gus Gussie
Aura (L) breeze. Aure
Aurea (L) golden
Aurelia (L) golden. Auriol
Aurora (Gk) dawn. Aurore

Autumn from the name of
the season
Ava see **Avis**
Avani (Sa) of the earth
Avara (Sa) young one
Aveline see **Evelyn**
Averil (OE) slayer of the
boar. Averill
Avis (L) bird. Ava Avice
Aviva (H) youthful. Avivi
Aviya
Awena (W) muse. Awen
Axelia (Gk) protector
Ayla (H) oak tree
Aysha (Af) life
Azaria (H) blessed by God
Aziza (A) cherished
Azura (F) blue

Bailey (F) steward
Bambi from the Italian
word *bambina* meaning
'baby girl'

Bano (A) woman
Baptista (L) baptised one.
Batista Battista Bautista
Baraka (A) blessing. Barakah
Barbara (Gk) stranger.
Babette Barbra
Basia (H) daughter of God.
Basha Basya
Basilia (Gk) regal. Basillia
Bathsheba (H) seventh
daughter. Batsheva
Bethsheba
Batya (H) daughter of God.
Basha Basia Basya Batyah
Beatrice (L) bringer of joy.
Bea Beatrix Bee Trixie
Bedelia (Ir) strong. Bedelie
Begonia (F) flowering plant
Belicia (Ir) dedicated to God.
Belica
Belina (F) goddess. Beline
Belinda (T) serpent – symbol
of wisdom. Linda Lindy
Belita (S) beautiful
Belle (F) beautiful. Bella
Bellona (L) Roman goddess
of war
Bena (H) wise woman

Benedicta (L) blessed.
  Benecia Benedetta
  Benedictina Benice Benicia
  Benita Benite Benoite
  Bettina
Benita (L) blessed. Benedicta
Berenice (Gk) bringer of
  victory. Bernice
Bernadette (F) bold as a
  bear. Bernadina Bernadine
Bertha (T) shining. Berta
  Berte Berthe
Berthilda (E) shining maid.
  Berthilde Bertilda
Berwyn (W) fair-haired one
Beryl (Gk) from the name of
  the jewel
Bethany from the town near
  Jerusalem. Beth
Bethseda (H) place of mercy
Beulah (H) married
Beverley (OE) from the
  beaver stream. Bev
  Beverly
Beyonce (NA) beyond others
Bianca Italian form of
  Blanche
Bibi (A) king's daughter, lady
Bibiana (L) lively. Bibbiana
Bidelia (Ir) high one, exalted
Bijou (F) jewel

Billie (OE) strong willed. Billy
Bina (Af) dancer
Bindu (Sa) pearl, truth
Birdy (OE) bird
Blaine (C) angular, thin
Blair (Ga) from the plain
Blaise (L) to stutter. Blase
  Blaze
Blanche (F) pale, fair. Bianca
Bliss (OE) joy
Blossom (OE) fragrant as a
  flower
Blowden (W) white flower
Blythe (OE) joyous. Blyth
Bo (Ch) precious
Bonita (S) pretty. Bonnie
Bonnie (Ga) beautiful. Bonny
Bracha (H) blessing
Braith (W) freckled
Branwen (W) dark, pure
Brede (E) from the open plains
Brenda (T) fire brand
Brenna (Ga) raven-haired
Briallen (W) primrose
Briana (Ga) strong
Brianne (C) female form of
  Brian
Bridget (Ga) resolute
  strength. Biddy Birgit
  Birgitta Bride Bridie Brigid
  Brigitte

Brier (OE) wild rose. Briar
Brina (Sl) protector
Briony see **Bryony**
Brittany (E) from Brittany
Bronwyn (W) white-breasted. Bronwen
Brooke (OE) reward. Brook
Brunella (F) dark-haired one. Brunelle Brunetta
Bryn (W) hill
Bryony (OE) twisting vine. Briony
Buffy originally a pet name for **Elizabeth**
Bunny (E) small rabbit
Bunty (E) little lamb

Cadence (I) rhythmic. Caddie Cadena Cadenza Cadina Cady
✗ **Caitlin** Irish form of **Katharine**
Cala (A) castle. Calla Callah
Calandra (Gk) lark. Callie

Calantha (Gk) beautiful flower. Calanthe Kalanthe
Caledonia (L) from Scotland
Caley (Ir) slender. Caleigh Kaley Kayley
Calida (S) warm
Callia (Gk) beautiful. Calla
Callidora (Gk) gift of beauty
Calliope (Gk) beautiful voice. Callie Cally Kaliope Kalliopi
Callista (Gk) most beautiful. Calista Calla
Callula (L) lovely girl, beautiful girl
Calpurnia (L) beautiful, lover
Caltha (L) yellow blossom
Calypso (Gk) concealer
Cameron (Ga) crooked nose. Camryn
Camilla (L) noble, righteous. Cam Camala Camile Kamala Millie
Canace (Gk) child of the wind
Candace (Gk) glittering. Candice Candis Candy
Candida (L) white. Candide Candy
Caprice (I) impulsive, capricious. Capri
Capucine (F) cape. Capicina Capucine

Cara (Ga) friend
Caradoc (W) friendly, amiable
Caraf (W) beloved
Caresse (F) loving touch, beloved. Caressa
Carina (L) keel. See also **Katharine**
Carissa (L) artful one. See also **Charity**
Carita (L) kind. Charity
Carla see **Caroline**
Carlotte Italian form of **Charlotte**
Carly see **Caroline**, **Charlotte**
Carma (Sa) destiny
Carmel (H) vineyard
Carmen (L) song. Charmain Charmaine Sharmaine
Carol see **Caroline**
Caroline (T) womanly. Carla Carleen Carlen Carlene Carlin Carly Carlyn Carol Carola Carole Carolin Carolina Carolyn Carrie Charlene Kararaina
Caron (F) pure. Carron
Carrie see **Caroline**
Carys (W) love
Cascata (I) waterfall

Casey (Ga) courageous. Casie
Casilda (L) one who loves their home
Cassandra (Gk) prophet. Cassie Sandy
Cassidy (Ir) love, esteem
Casta (Gk) perfect, pure
Catherine see **Katharine**
Ceana (Ir) God is good
Cecilia (L) blind, musical. Cecile Cecily Celia Celie Cicley Cissy Hihiria Sheela Sheelagh Sheila Shelley Sissy
Celandia (Gk) swallow (the bird)
Celena (Gk) dark
Celerina (S) lively, quick
Celeste (L) heavenly. Celestine
Celina (S) moon
Celine (F) sky, heaven. Celena
Cera (Ir) red. Ceara
Ceres (L) child of spring. Cerelia
Ceri (W) love. Cerian
Cerise (F) cherry. Cherise
Chalondra (Af) smart
Chana (H) gracious. Chanah
Chanda from the name of the element Chan

Chandler (F) candle maker
Chandra (Sa) moon-like
Chantal (F) singer
Charis (Gk) grace. Caris Carys
Charity (F) charitable.
    Carissa Cherry
Charlene see **Caroline**
Charlize (F) womanly,
    feminine
Charlotte (F) womanly.
    Carlotta Carlotte Carly
    Charlie Harata Hariata
    Gariata Lottie Lotty
    Sherry
Charmaine French form of
    Carmen
Charmian (Gk) a little joy
Charo (S) rose
Chastity (L) pure, virtuous
Chaviva (H) beloved
Chaya (H) life. Chava
Chelsea (OE) port
Chen (Ch) precious
Cher (F) beloved. Chere
    Cherie Cherish Sherry
Cherry (F) cherry-like. See
    also **Charity**
Cheryl (F) beloved. Sheryl
Chesna (Sl) peaceful
Chevonne (Ir) female form
    of Sean

Chiara (I) bright, light
Chimene (F) hospitable
Chiquita (S) little girl
Chloe (Gk) young green shoot
Chloris (Gk) blooming, fresh.
    Cloris
Christabel (L) beautiful
    Christian. Chris Christian
    Christiana Christie
    Christina Christine Christy
    Cristabel Crystal Kirsten
    Kirstin Kristin Kristy Tina
Christina, **Christine** see
    Christabel
Chruse (Gk) golden
Ciara (Ir) black-haired one.
    Ciaran
Cicley English form of
    Cecilia
Cindy see **Cynthia**, **Lucinda**
Cinnamon (H) cinnamon
Cira (I) sun
Clare (L) bright. Clair Claire
    Clara Clarice Clarissa
Clarinda (S) shining blossom
    of spring. Clorinda
Claudia (L) lame. Claudette
    Claudine Gladys
Clelia (Gk) glory
Clementine (L) merciful.
    Clemence Clementina

Cleo (Gk) famous
Cleopatra (Gk) glory of her father. Cleo Kleopatra
Cliantha (Gk) flower of glory
Clio (Gk) she who proclaims
Clodagh (Ir) from the name of the river in Tipperary
Clover (OE) clover blossom
Clydia (Gk) glorious
Cody (E) pillow, cushion. Codie Kody
Colette (F) victorious. Collette. See also **Nicola**
Colleen (Ga) girl
Conception (I) beginning. Concepcion Concepta Concetta Conchita
Concordia (L) harmony
Constance (L) constancy. Connie Constanta Constantia Constanzia
Consuela (S) free from sadness, console. Consolata Consuelo
Cora (Gk) maiden. Coretta Corinna Corinne
Coral (L) coral. Coralie
Corazon (S) from the heart
Cordelia (W) jewel of the sea. Cordelie Delia

Corey (Ir) from the hollow. Cory Korey
Corinne (F) maiden. Corina Corinna Corrina
Corliss (E) cheerful, kind
Cornelia (L) horn – symbol of royalty. Cornelie Nell
Cosette (F) victorious. Cozette
Cosima (Gk) female form of Cosmo
Courtenay (F) from the court. Courteney Courtnay Courtney
Creda (E) faith
Cressida (Gk) golden one
Crispina (L) with curly hair. Crispine
Crystal (L) clear as crystal. Christal Chrystal Cristal Krystal Krystle. See also **Christina**
Cwen (E) regal, queen
Cybil see **Sibyl**
Cyma (Gk) flourish
Cynara (Gk) thistle
Cynthia (Gk) the moon. Cindy
Cyrilla (Gk) proud one. Cirilla

Dacey (Ir) one from the south. Dacie Dacy Daycie

Dacia (Gk) from the ancient town of Dacia

Dae (E) day

Daffodil (Gk) name of a flower

Dagmar (T) glorious

Dairine (Ir) productive

Daisy (OE) day's eye. See also **Margaret**

Dakota (NA) allies

Dale (T) from the valley

Dallas (Ir) wise. Dalys

Damali (A) beautiful

Damaris (Gk) gentle. Dama Damara

Damiana (Gk) tame

Damita (S) noble lady, princess

Dana (T) from Denmark

Danica (Sl) the morning star

Danielle (H) God has judged. Danella Daniela Daniella Danila Danny

Daphne (Gk) laurel

Dara (H) compassion

Daralis (E) beloved

Darby (Ir) free. Derby

Darcy (Ir) dark. D'Arcey Darcey Darci Darcie

Daria (Gk) wealthy, queen

Darlene (OE) little darling. Darleen

Darra (Ir) small prosperous one

Darva (Sl) honey bee

Daryl (F) beloved. Darel, Darelle, Darryl

Davida (H) beloved, darling. Dava Davene Davina Davinia Davita Vida

Dawn (OE) daybreak

Daya (H) little bird

Dea (Gk) goddess

Deanna see **Diana**

Deborah (H) bee. Debbie Debora Debra Devora

Decima (Gk) tenth

Decla (Ir) female form of Declan

Dee (W) dark beauty

Deirdre (Ga) sorrow. Dedra Deidre

Delia (Gk) visible. See also **Cordelia**

Delicia (L) delight. Delica
  Delice Delissa Delizia
  Delysee
Delilah (H) temptress. Lila
  Lilah
Delma (S) from the sea.
  Delora
Delphine (L) dolphin. Delfa
  Delfina Delfine Delphina
  Delvene Delvine
Delwyn (W) neat. Delwen
Delyth (W) pretty
Dembe (Af) peace
Demi from the French word
  demi meaning 'half'
Dena (E) from the valley.
  Denna
Denise (Gk) wine lover. Denice
Derry (Ir) red-haired one
Dervila (Ir) poet's daughter
Desdemona (Gk) misery
Desiree (F) desired
Desma (Gk) pledge
Dessa (Gk) wanderer
Destiny from the French
  word *destin* meaning 'fate'
Deva (Sa) devine
Devin (Ir) poet
Dextra (L) skilful. Dex
Dhana (A) of the desert

Diamanta (F) cannot be
  conquered
Diana (L) moon goddess.
  Deana Deanna Diahann
  Dian Diane Dianna Dianne
  Riana
Diantha (Gk) heavenly
  flower. Dianthe
Diara (Af) gift
Diata (Af) lionness
Didina (F) desired
Dilys (W) true
Dinah (H) judged by law.
  Dina
Dione (Gk) daughter of
  heaven and earth. Dionne
Dita (L) lost
Diva (L) goddess. Divina
Dixie (F) tenth
Diza (H) joyous
Dobah (H) female bear
Dobrila (Sl) kind, good.
  Dobrana
Dodie (H) beloved. See also
  Dorothy
Dolly see **Dorothy**
Dolores (S) sorrowful. Lola
  Lolita
Dominga (S) Sunday

Dominica (L) belonging to the Lord. Domenica Domini Dominique

Donalda (E) leader. Donaldina Donelda

Donata (L) gift

Donatella (I) beautiful, star

Donna (I) lady

Dora see **Dorothy**

Dorcas (Gk) gazelle

Doreen (Ga) sullen

Dorinda (Gk) beautiful

Doris (Gk) nymph

Dorit (H) generation. Dorrit

Dorothy (Gk) gift of God. Dodie Dodo Dolly Dora Dorothea Dot Tarati

Dory (E) golden-haired

Dove (OE) bird

Drea (Gk) courageous

Dreama (Gk) joyful, happy music

Drina (S) defender, helper

Drisana (Sa) child of the sun

Drusilla (L) strong. Drew Dru

Duena (S) loyal

Dulcie (L) sweet. Dulcinea

Dulcina (L) rose. Dulcinea

Duvessa (Ir) dark beauty

Dyllis (W) sincere

Dymphna (Ir) fitting. Dympna

Dyna (Gk) powerful

Dysis (Gk) sunset

Earla (E) pledge. Earlene

Eartha (OE) of the earth

Easter (E) born at Easter

Eavan (Ir) fair one

Ebere (Af) merciful

Ebony (NA) black, hard wood

Ebrilla (W) April. Ebrel

Eda (E) rich. Edalene

Edana (Ir) fiery. Eidan

Edelyn (E) noble. Edlyn

Eden (H) delight

Edira (H) mighty

Edith (OE) rich gift. Ede Edie Edita

Edlin (E) princess. Edla Edlyn Edlynn Edlynne

Edmonda (E) wealthy protector. Edmunda

Edna (H) rejuvenation. Eddie

POPULAR BABY NAMES

This is a combined list of the most popular baby names in New Zealand in 2005 according to the Births, Deaths and Marriages Office of New Zealand.

Boys	*Girls*
Jack	Emma
Joshua	Ella
Samuel	Charlotte
Daniel	Olivia
James	Jessica
Benjamin	Sophie
Liam	Grace
William	Hannah
Ethan	Emily
Jacob	Isabella

Edria (H) mighty
Edsel (E) wealthy
Edwardina (E) wealthy
   guardian. Edwardine
Edwina (E) joyful companion.
   Edena
Eerma see **Irma**
Efia (Af) born on a Tuesday
Efrosini (H) fawn
Eglantine (L) prickly.
   Eglentyne
Ehetera Maori form of
   Esther
Eileen Irish form of **Evelyn**
Eira (W) snow
Eirian (W) silver. Eirianedd
   Eirianell
Eirlys (W) snowdrop
Eithne (Ir) fiery. Aithne Edna
   Ena Enya
Ekata (Sa) unity
Elain (W) fawn
Elaine Welsh form of **Helen**
Elan (W) to push
Elana (L) light. Elani
Elata (L) happy
Eldora (S) golden
Eleanor (Gk) bright. Eleanora
   Eleanore Elinor Elinore Ella
   Ellen Ellie Lenora Lenore
   Leonora Leonore Nell

Electra (Gk) brilliant
Eleora (H) one who follows
   the light of God
Elfrida (E) noble. Alfreda
   Elfreda
Eliane (L) sunshine. Eliana
Elin (Sc) light
Elina (Gk) intelligent
Elinor (E) light
Eliora (H) light of God. Eleora
Elise French form of
   Elizabeth
Elita (T) chosen
Elizabeth (H) my God is
   satisfaction. Babette Bess
   Bessie Bet Beth Betsey
   Betsy Bette Bettina Betty
   Buffy Elisabet Elisabeth
   Elise Elissa Eliza Elsa
   Elsbeth Else Elsie Elspeth
   Elyse Ihipera Irihapeti
   Isabel Isabella Isabelle
   Isobel Lib Libby Liesl Lilian
   Lisa Lisabeth Lise Lisette
   Lissa Liz Liza Lizabeth
   Lizzie Lizzy Ysabel
Elke (H) owned by God. Elkie
Ella (T) beautiful elf
Ellen see **Eleanor**, **Helen**
Ellie see **Eleanor**
Elma (Gk) pleasant

Elmira (E) noble
Elodie (OE) wealthy
Eloise (T) healthy. Helewise Heloise
Elon (Af) loved by God
Elora (Gk) light
Elpida (Gk) hope
Elsa German form of **Elizabeth**
Elsie, **Elspeth** see **Elizabeth**
Elva (Ga) Anglicised form of the Gaelic **Ailbhe**
Elvina (E) friend of the elves. Alvina Elva
Elvira (S) fair, blonde one
Elwyne (W) pale, fair
Elysia (L) divinely happy
Eman (A) faithful
Emanuele (F) Emanuela Emanuelle
Emele (F) hard-working, admirable. Emera
Emeline French form of **Amelia**
Emerald (E) precious jewel
Emily (T) industrious. Emilia
Emma (T) universal
Emmanuelle (H) God is with me. Emanuelea Emanuelle Emmanuelea Manuela
Emuna (A) faith. Iman

Ena (Ir) fiery. Aine Enya
Endora (H) fountain
Enid (W) purity
Enola (NA) magnolia
Enora (Gk) light
Eranthe (Gk) springtime flower
Erasma (Gk) easygoing, amiable
Erica (N) ruler. Erika
Erin (Ga) from Ireland. Erinna
Ernestine (T) vigorous. Erna Ernesta Ernestina
Eshana (Sa) one who searches
Esme (F) esteemed. Edme Esmee
Esmeralda Spanish form of **Emerald**
Esperanza (S) hope. Esperance
Esta (I) one who comes from the east
Estelle (F) star
Esther (H) myrtle. Ehetera Hadassah Hester Hetty
Estralita (S) little star
Estrella (S) star
Etain (Ir) shining. Etan
Etana (H) dedication

Ethel (OE) noble
Etienette (F) garland, crown
Etoile (F) star
Etta see **Henrietta**
Eucaria (Gk) happy helper.
  Euchar Eucharya
Euclea (Gk) glorious
Eudora (Gk) happy gift
Eudoxia (Gk) happy, glory.
  Eudocie Eudokhia Eudossia
  Eudoxie
Eugenia (Gk) noble. Eugenie
Eulalia (Gk) sweetly speaking
Eunice (Gk) great victory
Euphemia (Gk) auspicious
  speech
Euphrasia (Gk) joy, delight
Eustacia (Gk) fruitful
Eva see **Eve**
Evadne (Gk) fortunate one
Evangeline (Gk) harbinger
  of good news. Eva
  Evangelina Eve
Evania (Gk) untroubled
Eve (Gk) lively. Eva Evie
Evelien (F) life
Evelyn (T) pleasant. Aileen
  Aveline Eileen Evelina
Evonne see **Yvonne**

Fabia (L) bean grower
Fabrianne (L) resourceful.
  Fabriane Farbrienne
Fahima (A) intelligent
Faine (E) joyous. Faina Fayne
Fairley (E) clearing. Fairlee
  Fairleigh Fairlie
Faith (T) fidelity. Fay Faye
Faizah (Af) victorious
Faline (L) cat-like
Fallon (Ga) grandchild of the
  ruler
Fancy (Gk) to see. Fancie
Fanny see **Frances**
Fantine (F) child-like
Fareeda (A) unique
Faren (E) wanderer. Faran
  Farin
Farfalla (I) butterfly
Farrah (OE) beautiful,
  pleasant. Farah
Fathia (A) victory
Fatima (A) creator. Fatimah
Faustine (I) fortunate.
  Fausta Faustina
Fauve (F) wild

Fawn (F) young deer
Fay (F) fairy. Faye. See also **Faith**
Fayre (E) fair
Feenat (Ir) deer
Fei (Ch) empress, regal
Felicia (L) happy, lucky. Felicie Felicity
Fenella (Ga) white-shouldered. Finola Fionnuala Fionnula
Fern (OE) fern
Fernanda (T) adventurous
Fidela (L) faithful. Faith Fidelia Fidelity
Fifi French form of **Josephine**
Filma (E) misty veil
Filomena (Gk) harmony. Philomena
Fina (Ir) Anglicised form of the Gaelic **Fiona**. Finna
Finella (Ir) white-shouldered. Fenella Finola
Fiona (Ga) white
Fiorella (I) small flower. Fiorenza
Flair (Ir) with style. Flaire
Flannery (F) flat piece of metal. Flann Flanna
Flavia (L) fair-haired

Flax (E) from the name of the plant
Fleur (F) flower
Flora (L) flower. Floria
Florence (L) blooming. Flo Florrie Flossie Floy
Flos (N) leader
Fontaine (F) spring, fountain
Fortuna (L) luck
Fossetta (F) dimpled
Frances (L) Frenchwoman. Fanny Fran Francesca Francie Francine Francoise Frankie Frannie
Freda (T) peaceful. Frieda. See also **Winifred**
Frederica (T) peaceful ruler
Freya (Sc) noble woman. Freyja
Fulvia (L) golden-haired
Fuscienne (L) dark, black

Gabrielle (H) strong woman of God. Gabey Gabriel Gabriela Gabriella Gaby

Gada (H) lucky, fortunate
Gaea (Gk) the earth. Gaia
Gaenor see **Guenevere**
Gail pet form of **Abigail**
Gala (I) finery
Galatea (Gk) milky white
Gale (Ir) stranger
Galina (Gk) calm. Galena
  Halina
Gamada (Af) pleased
Gana (H) garden. Ganya
Garland (F) crown of
  blossoms
Garnet (OE) deep red gem.
  Garnette
Gay (Fr) lively, merry. Gai
  Gaylene
Gayle see **Abigail**
Gaylor (F) brave
Gaynor see **Guenevere**
Gemina (Gk) twin. Geminie
Gemma (I) precious stone
Gena (F) Gene Genna
Geneva (Fr) juniper tree. Gene
Genevieve (F) white wave.
  Gena Genie Jenny
Georgeanne combination of
  George and **Anne**
Georgina (Gk) farmer.
  Georgia Georgiana Georgie
  Gina

Geraldine (T) noble spear-
  carrier. Dina Geralda
  Gerardine Gerhardine
  Gerry Jerry
Geranium (L) from the name
  of the flower
Gerda (Sc) protected. Garda
Germaine (L) from Germany
Gersemi (Sc) jewel
Gertrude (T) spear-carrier.
  Trudy
Gianna (I) God is good.
  Gianina Giovanna
Gilda (OE) golden
Gillian (L) downy. Gill Jill
  Jillian. See also **Julia**
Gina see **Georgina**, **Regine**
Ginevra Italian form of
  Guenevere
Ginger see **Virginia**
Giselle (T) pledge. Gisela
  Gisele
Gitel (H) goodness. Gittel
Githa (N) warrior. Gytha
Gladys (W) ruler. See also
  Claudia
Glenda see **Glenna**
Glenna (C) from the valley.
  Glenda Glennis Glenys
  Glynis

Glenys (W) pure. Gleni
Gleníce Glennis
Gloria (L) glorious
Glynis see **Glenna**
Godiva (OE) gift of God
Golda (OE) golden. Goldie
Grace (L) graceful. Gracie
Grainne (Ga) love. Grania
Greer (Gk) watchful
Greta Swedish form of
Margaret
Gretchen German form of
Margaret
Griselda (T) grey warrior.
Grisel Grize Grizel Zelda
Guadalupe (S) from the river
of the wolf. Lupe
Gudron (Sc) divine. Gudrun
Guenevere (W) white.
Gaenor Gaynor Ginevra
Guinevere Gwen Jenifer
Jennifer Jenny
Gunhilda (N) maiden of
battle. Gonnilda Gunda
Gunnhild
Gurit (H) innocent
Gussie (W) see **Augusta**
Gustava (Sc) rod of the gods

Gwendolyn (W) white-
browed. Guendolen Gwen
Gwenda Gwendoline Gwyn
Gwynne Wendy
Gwylan (W) seagull
Gwyneth (W) white, blessed.
Gwyn Venetia Winnie
Gypsy (E) wanderer. Gipsy
Gytha (E) gift

Hadassah see **Esther**
Hadley (E) from the field of
heather. Hadleigh
Hafwen (W) beautiful like a
summer's day
Hagar (H) forsaken one. Hajar
Haidee (Gk) modest
Haki Maori form of **Jackie**
Halcyon (Gk) kingfisher.
Halcyone
Hale (E) heroic. Hailey
Haleigh Haley Halie
Halima (Af) gentle
Halley (E) surname meaning
'dweller of the meadow'

Hallie (Gk) one who thinks of the sea

Halona (NA) happy fortune. Halonna

Hannah (H) God has favoured me. Hana Hanna Hanni

Haralda (E) ruler. Harelda Harolda Haroldina

Harata, **Hariata** Maori form of **Charlotte**

Harley (E) from the meadow. Harleigh Harlene

Harmony (E) harmony. Harmonia

Harper (E) harp player

Harriet (T) ruler of the estate. Hariette Hatty

Hava (H) life

Havana (S) place of refuge. Havanna Havannah

Hayley (OE) hay maiden. Hailey Haley

Hazel (E) hazel tree

Heather (E) heather

Hebe (Gk) youth

Heidi (T) noble, kind

Helen (Gk) bright one. Alaina Elaine Eleni Elle Ellen Ellie Galina Helena Helene Ilona Lanie Lena Nell

Helga see **Olga**

Helia (Gk) sun

Helianthe (Gk) bright, colourful flower

Helise (Gk) spiral. Helice

Heloise see **Eloise**

Hene Maori form of **Jane**

Henrietta (T) ruler of the estate. Etta Hatty Henriette Hettie Yetta

Hephzibah (H) my delight is in her. Hephsibah Hepzibah

Hera Maori form of **Sarah**

Hermione (Gk) of the earth

Hermosa (S) beautiful

Hesper (Gk) evening star. Hespera Hesperia

Hester see **Esther**

Hibernia (L) from Ireland

Hibiscus (Gk) from the name of the tropical flower

Hihiria Maori form of **Cecilia**

Hilary (L) cheerful. Hillary

Hilda (OE) warrior

Hollis surname meaning 'dweller of the holly trees'

Holly (E) holly plant

Honey (E) honey. See also **Honora**

Honora (L) beautiful, honourable. Honey Honoria Nora Norah Noreen

Hope (E) hope
Horatia (L) time keeper
Hortense (L) gardener.
  Hortensia
Hosanna (L) praise God.
  Hosana
Hua (Ch) flower
Huette (F) of the heart and
  mind. Huela Huguette
Huhana Maori form of **Susan**
Huia (M) from the name of
  the bird
Hune Maori form of **June**
Hunter (E) hunter,
  sportsman
Huria Maori form of **Julia**
Hyacinth (Gk) from the name
  of the flower. Giacinta
  Jacinta Jacinth
Hypatia (Gk) highest one

Ianthe (Gk) violet flower.
  Iona Ione
Ida (T) hard-working

Idala (H) one who walks
  softly
Idonea (N) goddess of
  spring. Idona
Idra (H) fig, flag
Idris (Ir) fiery
Ignatia (L) fiery. Ignacia
  Ignazia
Ihipera Maori form of **Isabel**
Ila (F) from the island
Ilana (H) big tree
Ilka (Ga) each and every one
Ilona Hungarian form of
  Helen
Ilyssa (H) thoughtful,
  mindful
Imala (NA) tough, strong
Imelda (OE) moderate
Immaculada (S) of the
  immaculate conception
Imogen (C) daughter.
  Imogene Innagen Innogen
Imperia (L) imperial one.
  Imperio
India from the name of the
  country
Indu (Sa) moon
Inez Spanish form of **Agnes**
Inge (Sc) daughter of a hero.
  Inga Ingaborg

Ingrid (N) hero's daughter.
Inga Inge
Iola (Gk) dawn cloud
Iolanthe Greek form of
Violet
Ionia (Gk) name of an
ancient region
Ionna (Gk) a gift from God
Iorwen (W) beautiful
Iphigenia (Gk) the daughter
of Agamemnon
Iram (A) heavenly
Irene (Gk) peace. Irena Irina
Irihapeti Maori form of
Elizabeth
Iris (Gk) rainbow
Irma (Gk) noble. Erma
Irvette (E) from the sea
✱**Isabel** French and Spanish
form of **Elizabeth**
Isabis (Af) beautiful
Isadora (Gk) gift. Isidora
Isi (NA) deer, child of God
Isla (F) from the island. Ila
Isola (I) isolated, island
Isolda (T) ice ruler
Ita (Ga) desire for truth
Iva (F) yew tree
Ivana (H) God is good. Evana
Ivanka Ivanna
Ivory (E) ivory

Ivy (E) ivy
Izora (A) dawn

Jacinda (Gk) beautiful.
Jacenda
Jacinth French form of
Hyacinth
Jackie see **Jacqueline**
Jacoba (H) to supplant
or conquer. Jacobella
Jacobina Jacovina Jakoba
Jakuba
Jacqueline (H) supplanter.
Haki Jackie Jacoba
Jacobina Jacquelyn
Jacquetta Jaquetta
Jada (H) wise
Jade (L) precious jewel
Jael (H) one who ascends
the mountain. Yael
Jaffa (H) beautiful, lovely.
Yaffa
Jaime (F) to love. Jaimee
Jala (A) charitable
Jaleela (A) honour. Jalila

Jalena (Sl) light
Jalia (A) great one
Jama (Sa) daughter
Jamari (F) great girl warrior
Jamie female form of James.
　Jaime
Jamila (Af) beautiful
Jane (H) God is gracious.
　Hene Jan Jana Janet
　Janeta Janette Janice
　Janina Janine Janis Jayne
　Jean Jeanette Jenny Joan
　Joanna Joanne Johanna
　Joni Sheena Shena Shona
　Sine Sinead Siobhan Vania
　Vanya
Janet see **Jane**
Janice American form of
　Jane
Janna (H) to flourish and
　thrive
Japonica (L) a flowering tree
Jara (Sl) spring (the season)
Jarita (Sa) bird
Jarmila (Sa) spring (the
　season)
Jasmin (P) fragrant flower.
　Jasmine Jessamine Yasmin
Javeira (S) one who owns a
　new home. Javeera
Jay (OE) blue jay

Jaya (Sa) victory. Jayanti
Jaylene modern combination
　using **Jay**
Jean, **Jeannette** Scottish
　forms of **Jane**
Jemima (H) dove. Jem
　Jemimah Jemma
Jena (A) paradise
Jennifer Cornish form of
　Guenevere
Jenny see **Genevieve**,
　Guenevere, **Jane**
Jeno (Gk) heaven-sent
Jensine (H) God is kind
Jereni (Sl) peace
Jessenia (A) flower
Jessica (H) he beholds.
　Jessie
Jet (L) black. Jetta
Jewel (F) jewel, precious
　stone
Jezebel (H) wicked
Jill see **Gillian**
Jina (Gk) farmer. Jirina
Jinx (L) spell
Joan, **Joanna**, **Joanne** see
　Jane
Jobina (H) persecuted. Jobey
　Jobie Joby
Jocasta (Gk) mother of
　Oedipus

Jocelyn (L) playful. Joscelin Joscelyn Joss Joyce

Jocosa (L) playful

Jodie see **Judith**

Joelle (F) Jehovah is God. Joella Joelly Joely

Johari (Af) jewel

Jola (Gk) pretty

Jolie (F) pretty

Jonina (H) dove of peace. Joni Jonita

Jonquil (L) from the name of the flower

Jordan (H) flowing down. Jordana

Josephine (H) God shall add. Fifi Jo Joey Jolene Josepha Josette Josie

Jovanna (L) majestic. Giovanna Jeovana Jeovanna

Jovita (L) joyful, jovial. Jovena Joveta Jovi

Joy (F) rejoice. Joyce

Joyce see **Jocelyn**, **Joy**

Joyita (S) jewel

Juanita (S) girl of God. Juana Nita

Jubilee (H) celebration

Jucosa (L) jocular, playful

Judith (H) Jewish. Jodie Jody Jude Judi Judie Judy Turuhira

Judy see **Judith**, **Julia**

Julia (L) youthful. Gill Gillian Huria Jill Jillian Judy Julian Juliana Julianne Julie Julienne Juliet Juliette

Julinka (L) young one

Jumana (A) pearl

Jun (Ch) truthful

June (L) from the name of the month. Hune

Juniper from the name of the berry

Juno (L) queen of heaven

Jurisa (Sl) Stormy

Justina (L) just. Justine Justy

Jyoti (Sa) light

Kabibe (Af) little girl

Kabira (A) powerful

Kacela (Af) hunter

30

Kadisha (H) holy
Kaela (A) beloved. Kaelah
  Kayla Keyla
Kaila (H) laurel, crown
Kaina (W) beautiful
Kainda (Af) daughter of a
  hunter
Kala (Ha) sun. Kalama
✳ **Kali** (Sa) energy
Kalida (A) eternal one.
  Khalida
Kalika (Gk) rosebud
Kalila (A) beloved
Kalinda (Sa) view, sun.
  Kalynda
Kaliope (Gk) beautiful.
  Callipe
Kalista (Gk) most beautiful.
  Callista
Kallan (Sc) flowing water
Kama (Sa) love
Kamana (Sa) desire
Kamania (Af) like the moon
Kamaria (Af) child of the
  moon
Kambo (Af) hard worker
Kamila (A) perfect
Kamilia (Sl) perfumed
  flower, sweet one
Kamin (Sa) joyful
Kanani (Ha) beauty

Kane (Ir) beautiful fighter
Kanta (Sa) beautiful,
  desirable
Kara (Gk) pure. Cara
Kararaina Maori form of
  Caroline
Karas (Gk) grace, beauty
Karen Danish form of
  Katharine
Karida (A) pure, virginal.
  Kareeda
Karima (A) generous
Karis (Gk) graceful. Karice
  Karise
Karma (Sa) destiny, fate,
  star
Kasimira (Sl) one who
  demands peace
Kassidy (Ir) clever. Kassie
Katarina Maori form of
  Katharine, **Catherine**
Katharine (Gk) pure. Caitlin
  Carina Caryn Catarina
  Caterina Catherina
  Catherine Cathleen
  Cathy Catriona Ekaterina
  Karen Karin Katarina
  Kate Katerina Katherine
  Kathleen Kathryn Kathy
  Katie Katrina Katrine
  Katya Kay Kit Kitty Taryn

ROYAL NAMES

Boys	*Girls*
Albert	Alexandra
Alexander	Anastasia
Alfred	Anne
Arthur	Beatrice
Charles	Catherine
Edmund	Diana
Edward	Elizabeth
Edwin	Finnuala
Ferdinand	Isabelle
George	Jane
Harry, Harold	Josephine
Henry	Louisa
James	Margaret
Louis	Marie
Nicholas	Mary
Phillip	Olivia
Richard	Rose
Vladimir	Sophia
William	Victoria

Kathleen Irish form of **Katharine**

Kay see **Katharine**

Kayla (Ir) slender

Kayleen (H) beloved. Kaileen Kaylene

Kayleigh (E) pure one. Kailey Kaley Kay Kayley

Keely (Ga) beautiful

Keena (Ir) brave

Keilani (Ha) leader. Keilana

Keisha (Af) most favoured

Kelda (N) deep, still water

Kelila (H) garland, laurel. Kelilah

Kella (Ir) warrior

Kelly (Ga) warrior

Kelsey (Sc) from the island

Kenda (Af) water baby. Kendie Kendy

Kendall (E) bright valley. Kendal Kendel Kendell

Kendra (OE) wise

Kenna (Ga) female form of Ken

Kennice (E) beautiful. Kanna Kenice Kenise Kennis Kennise

Kera (Ir) pure

Kerry (Ga) dark-haired. Keri Kiri

Keshia (Af) favourite. Beloved

Kesia (Af) favourite

Kestrel (F) rattle

Ketifa (A) to pick a flower

Ketina (H) girl

Keyna (W) jewel

Kia (Af) start of the season

Kiana (Ir) ancient one

Kiera (Ir) dark-haired. Ciara Ciera Keara Keira Kira

Kilmeny (Ir) stone kiln

Kim (OE) ruler

Kimberley (OE) from the royal meadow. Kim Kimberly

Kingsley (E) king's place.

Kinsey (E) young one. Kinsee

Kirby (N) church village. Kirbie

Kiri (M) tree bark. See also **Kerry**

Kirmi (Sa) golden image

Kirsten Scandinavian form of **Christine**

Kisha (Sl) rain

Kismet (A) fate

Kitra (H) crowned one

Kitri (S) small bird

Kiva (H) protected

Kolina (Gk) pure, young girl

Kora (Gk) maiden. Cora
  Koren Korene Kori
Kuini Maori form of **Queenie**
Kumani (Af) destiny
Kumari (Sa) daughter
Kundara (Sa) jasmine
Kyla (Ga) female form of
  Kyle
Kylie (Au) boomerang
Kyna (Ir) wise
Kyrene (Gk) noble ruler
Kyrie (Ir) dark-haired

La Tasha see **Natasha**
Lacey see **Larissa**
Ladelia (H) devoted to God.
  Lael
Ladonna (NA) lady
Laella (E) little elf
Lainey (F) wool. Laine
Lais (Gk) rejoice
Lakia (A) treasured
Lakota (NA) friend
Lakshmi (Sa) wealth, beauty
Lala (Sl) tulip. Lalla

Lalage (L) gentle laughter
Lalas (Sa) love
Lalita (Sa) charming
Lamis (A) soft
Lamora (F) honourable
Lana see **Alana**
Lane (E) lane, narrow
  country road
Lani (Ha) sky
Lanie (Gk) shortened form of
  Elaine
Lara (L) famous
Laraine see **Lorraine**
Larina (L) girl of the sea.
  Larine
Larissa (Gk) cheerful. Lacey
Lark (OE) skylark
Latania (F) queen of the
  fairies
Lateefah (A) kind. Latifah
Latisha (L) happy
Latoya (S) victory
Laura (L) bay tree. Laurel
  Lauren Lauretta Laurie
  Lora Loren Loretta Lori
Laveda (L) pure
Lavender (L) from the name
  of the flowering plant
Laverne (F) spring-like.
  Verna

Lavinia (L) daughter of Latinus
Lavonne (F) wood
Lawn grassed area
Layla (Af) born at night
Layna (Gk) light, truth
Leah (H) weary. Lea Lee Lia
Leala (F) faithful
Leandra (L) like a lioness
Leanne combination of **Lee** and **Anne**
Lece (F) happy. Lecia
Leda (Gk) lady
Lee (OE) from the meadow. Lea Leigh
Leena (Sa) devoted one. Lina
Leila (P) dark oriental beauty
Leilani (Ha) flower
Lena see **Helen**, **Madeline**
Lenita (L) gentle
Lenore see **Eleanor**
Leocadia (S) clear
Leonie (F) like a lioness. Leona Leontine
Leonora see **Eleanor**
Leora (Gk) light. Leor Liora
Lesley (Ga) from the grey fort. Leslie
Letitia (L) gladness. Laetitia Leta Lettice Letty

Levana (L) rising sun. Levania Levanna Livana
Levina (E) bright light
Lewanna (H) pure as the white moon
Li (Ch) plum blossom
Lian (Ch) willow tree
Liana (H) climbing vine. Leana Leane Leanna Liane Lianna Lianne
Libby Scottish form of **Elizabeth**
Liberty (L) freedom
Lila see **Delilah**
Lilian (L) lily, purity. Lillian Lillie Lily. See also **Elizabeth**
Lilith (A) goddess of storms
Lily (L) from the name of the flower. Lil Lillie. See also **Lilian**
Lina (A) tender
Linda (T) serpent. Lindy Lynda. See also **Melinda**
Lindsay (OE) linden tree. Lindsey Linsey Lyndsay
Ling (Ch) delicate
Linley (E) from the flax field. Lynley
Linnet see **Lynnette**
Liora (H) light

Lirit (Gk) lyre
Liron (H) happy in song.
   Lirone
Lisa, **Lise**, **Liz**, **Liza**, **Lizzy** see
   Elizabeth
Lissa see **Melissa**
Liv (N) protector, life
Livia (L) grey. Liviya
Livona (H) spice
Lobelia (L) from the name of
   the flower. Loelia
Lodema (E) leader
Lois (Gk) better. See also
   Louisa
Lola (Gk) see **Dolores**, **Louisa**
Lolita see **Dolores**
Lora see **Laura**
Lore (S) flower
Lorelei (T) alluring. Loralie
Loretta (I) crowned with
   laurels
Lori see **Laura**
Loris (Gk) pale
Lorna (E) from Lorne
Lorraine (T) famous in
   battle. Laraine Loraine
Lottie see **Charlotte**
Lotus (Gk) from the name of
   the flower

Louisa (T) famous warrior.
   Lois Lola Louie Louise Lulu
   Ruiha
Loveday (E) dear day. Love
   Lovette Lovisa
Lucia (I) light. Luca Luciana
   Lucianna Lucina Luzia
Lucilla, **Lucille**, **Lucinda** see
   Lucy
Lucretia (L) riches. Lucrece
Lucy (L) light. Lucia Luciana
   Lucilla Lucille Lucinda
   Ruha Ruihi
Ludmilla (Sl) loved by
   people. Ludmila
Luella (E) elfin, famous
Lula (A) pearl
Luna (L) moon
Lydia (Gk) from Lydia. Lidia
Lyla (F) from the island. Lila
Lynnette (F) linnet bird.
   Linnet Lyn Lynette Lynn
   Lynne
Lyra (Gk) lyre. Lyris
Lysandra (Gk) liberator.
   Lisandra

Maata Maori form of
   Martha
Mab (Ir) joyous
Mabel English form of
   Amabel
Macaria (Gk) happy
Mackenzie (Ir) fair,
   handsome
Madelia (Gk) from the high
   tower
Madeline (H) woman of
   Magdala. Lena Lina
   Maddie Madeleine
   Madelena Madge Magda
   Magdalen Magdalena
   Magdalene Makarena
   Marlene
Madge see **Madeline**,
   Margaret
Madhur (Sa) sweet
Madison (E) surname
   meaning 'Mad's son'
Madonna (I) my lady
Madra (S) mother. Madre
Madrona (L) noblewoman.
   Matrona Madra

Mae see **May**
Maedea (Gk) cunning
Maeve (Ga) legendary Queen
   of Connacht. Meave
Magda, **Magdalen** see
   Madeline
Maggie see **Margaret**
Magna (L) great one
Magnolia (E) magnolia
Maha (A) Great light
Mahala (H) affection.
   Mahalah Mahalia
Mahina (Ha) moon
Mahira (H) energetic
Maia (Gk) the eldest and most
   lovely of the Pleiades. Maya
Maida (OE) maiden
Maisie see **Margaret**
Majesta (L) majestic
Makarena Maori form of
   Magdalen, **Madeline**
Makareta, **Makareti**,
   Makere Maori forms of
   Margaret
Malati (Sa) jasmine flower
Malka (H) queen
Mallory (F) wearer of
   armour
Malva (Gk) soft. Melva
Malvina (T) chieftain.
   Malvinia Melva Melvina

Mamie see **Margaret**
Manat (A) fate
Manju (Sa) beautiful one
Manon French form of **Mary**
Manu (M) bird, kite
Manuela (S) God is with us
Mara (H) bitter. Marah
Marcia (L) warlike. Marcie
  Marsha
Mare from the name of the
  female horse
Margaret (Gk) pearl. Daisy
  Greta Gretchen Madge
  Maggie Maisie Makareta
  Makareti Makere Mamie
  Margareta Mararita
  Marge Margery Margie
  Margo Margot Margret
  Marguerita Marguerite
  Marjorie Marjory Markera
  Meg Megan Peg Peggy
  Rita
Margery French form of
  Margaret
Margo, **Margot**, **Marguerite**
  French forms of **Margaret**
Maria Italian form of **Mary**
Mariah see **Mary**
Marian combination of **Mary**
  and **Ann**. Marianne Marion
Marie French form of **Mary**

Mariel German form of **Mary**
Mariella (I) diminutive of
  Maria, Marietta
Marigold (E) from the name
  of the flower
Marilyn American form of
  Mary
Marina (L) from the sea.
  Marnie
Marion see **Mary**
Marjorie French form of
  Margaret
Marlene see **Madeline**
Marley (E) from the meadow
Marnie see **Marina**
Marsha see **Marcia**
Martha (A) lady. Maata
  Marta Marthe Marty Mata
  Matty
Martine (L) warlike. Martina
  Tina
Mary (H) wished-for child.
  Maidie Mair Manon Maria
  Mariah Marie Mariel
  Marietta Marilyn Marion
  Marlo Marnie Marya
  Masha Maure Maureen
  Mere Meri Mimi Miriam
  Miriama Mitzi Moira Moire
  Molly Moyra Pare Polly
Marya (A) purity

38

Mata Maori form of **Martha**

Matilda (T) mighty in battle.
Mathilda Matty Maud
Maude Tilda Tilly

Mattea (H) gift from God.
Matthea Mattia

Matty see **Martha**, **Matilda**

Maude see **Matilda**

Maure, **Maureen** Irish forms
of **Mary**

Maurelle (F) dark

Mavis (F) song, thrush

Maxine (L) the greatest.
Maxie

Maxy female form of Max

May (E) from the name of
the month. Mae Mei

Maya (Sa) illusion. Maia

Meara (Ga) mirth

Mee (Ch) beautiful. Mei

Meena (S) female saint

Meg, **Megan** see **Margaret**

Megara (Gk) first

Mei Maori form of **May**

Melanie (Gk) black. Melany
Melloney

Melba (E) mallow flower

Melina (Gk) gentle, song

Melinda (Gk) mild, gentle.
Linda

Melissa (Gk) honeybee

Melody (E) melody

Melva see **Malvina**

Mercedes (S) Mary of
Mercies

Mercy (E) mercy

Mere, **Meri** Maori forms of
Mary

Meredith (W) protector of
the sea

Meriel see **Muriel**

Merivale (E) beautiful valley

Merle (L) blackbird. Merrill
Meryl

Meta (Gk) wise

Mia (I) mine

Michelle (H) like the Lord.
Michaela Michal Michele
Micheline Micky

Mietta (F) small sweet girl

Mignon (F) delicate

Miguela (S) who can
compare to God? Miguelita

Mila (Sl) lovable. Milana

Milagros (S) miracles

Mildred (OE) strong worker.
Millie

Mimi see **Mary**

Mimosa (F) from the name
of the flower

Minerva (L) wisdom

Minette (F) faithful one.
   Minnette
Minna (T) small
Mira (L) wonderful. Mirabel
Mirabelle (L) wonderful.
   Mirabel Mirabella
Miranda (L) admired
Miriam see **Mary**
Misty (E) modern name,
   misty, foggy. Misti Mistie
Mitzi see **Mary**
Moana (Ha) ocean
Modesty (L) modest.
   Modestine
Mohini (Sa) enchantress
Moira, **Molly**, **Moyra** Irish
   forms of **Mary**
Mona (Ga) noble. Moyna
Monica (L) adviser. Monika
   Monique
Montana from the name of
   the US State
Morag (Ga) little sun
Morgan (W) from the sea.
   Morgana
Moriah (H) God is my teacher
Morna (Ga) beloved. Myrna
Moselle (H) from the water
Munira (A) brilliant
Murali (Sa) flute
Muriel (C) sea-bright. Meriel

Musa (L) muse. Musetta
   Musette Musidora
Myfanwy (W) my fine one.
   Miffany Myvanwy
Myrna see **Morna**
Myrtle (Gk) from the name
   of the shrub. Mertle

Nabila (A) noble. Nabeela
Nada (A) generous
Nadia Slavic form of **Nadine**
Nadine (F) hope. Nadia
Nadira (A) precious
Nagida (H) noblewoman
Naida (Gk) water nymph.
   Naia
Naila (A) successful
Naima (A) comfort
Naimah (A) happiness
Najette (F) clever
Nalani (Ha) calm and
   heavenly skies
Nalini (Sa) lovely
Nan, **Nancy** see **Ann**

Nana (Ha) spring (the season)
Nani (Gk) charming
Naomh (Ir) saint
Naomi (H) pleasant
Nara (E) near one
Narcissa (F) daffodil. Narcisse
Nasia (H) miracle from God. Naysa
Nata (Sa) dancer
Natalie (L) Christmas Day. La Tasha Natalia Natalya Natasha
Natasha Russian form of **Natalie**
Nathania (H) gift from God. Natania
Nayana (Sa) one with beautiful eyes
Neala (Ir) champion. Neela Neila
Neda (Sl) born on a Sunday
Nediva (H) noble
Neha (Sa) rain
Neige (F) snow
Nell see **Cornelia**, **Eleanor**, **Helen**
Nenet (E) goddess of the deep. Nene
Neola (Gk) young one

Neoma (Gk) new moon
Nerina (I) black
Nerine (Gk) sea nymph
Nerissa (Gk) of the sea
Neroli Gk) orange blossom. Nerolia Nerolie
Nerys (W) lord
Nessie, **Nest**, **Nesta** Welsh forms of **Agnes**
Neva (S) snowy
Nevada from the name of the US State
Nevina (Ir) worshipper. Nivena
Ngaio (M) from the name of the tree
Ngaire (M) flax. Nyree
Nia (Ir) beautiful
Niam (Ir) luminous. Niamh
Nicola (Gk) victory of the people. Collette Nichola Nicole Nicolette
Nima (A) bless
Nina Russian form of **Ann**
Nissa (Sc) friendly elf
Nita (NA) bear
Noel (F) born on Christmas Day. Noele Noella Noelle
Noelani (Ha) girl from heaven
Nola Irish form of **Olivia**
Nona (L) ninth

Noor (A) light
Nora, **Norah**, **Noreen** Irish
  forms of **Honora**
Norma (L) rule, pattern
Nova (L) new
Novia (S) sweetheart
Nuala (Ir) fair-shouldered
  one. Nola Nula
Nunciata (L) messenger.
  Nuncia
Nureen (A) light
Nydia (L) refuge
Nympha (Gk) nymph, bride
Nyree see **Ngaire**
Nyssa (Gk) beginning
Nyx (Gk) of the night

Obelia (Gk) marker, obelisk
Oceana modern name
  derived from the word
  ocean
Octavia (L) eighth child
Odeda (H) courageous
Odelia (T) prosperous

Odessa (Gk) long journey.
  Odyssey
Odette, **Odile** French forms
  of **Ottilia**
Odile (F) wealthy. Odela
  Odele Odilia
Ofira (H) gold. Ophira
Ofra (E) gift
Okalani (Ha) heavenly
Ola (Sc) descendant
Olethea (L) truth
Olga (Sc) holy. Helga
Olinda (L) fragrant. Olynda
Olivia (L) olive. Livia Livvie
  Nola Oliva Olive
Olwyn (W) white track.
  Olwen
Olympia (Gk) from Mt
  Olympus, the home of the
  gods
Oma (A) long life
Omega (Gk) final
Ondine see **Undine**
Oneida (NA) standing rock
Oni (Af) desirable
Oona, **Oonagh** Irish forms
  of **Una**
Opal from the name of the
  jewel
Ophelia (Gk) serpent
  – symbol of wisdom

Oprah (H) fawn. Ofra Ophra
  Ophrah Orpah
Ora (L) golden light. Gold
Orchid (L) from the name of
  the flower. Orchio
Oriana (L) golden
Oriel (L) golden. Aurelia
Orinda (H) type of pine tree
Oriole (L) fair-haired
Orla (Ir) golden. Orlaith
  Orlah
Orna (H) light
Ornella (I) type of tree.
  Ornette Ornice
Orsina (I) flowering ash
  tree
Ortensia (I) garden.
  Hortensia Ortense
Osanna (L) praise God
Ottilia (T) home lover. Odette
  Odile
Ova (L) egg
Owena (W) noble, young
  warrior. Oweena
Oz (H) strong
Ozara (H) wealth, treasure

Paca (L) tranquil
Pachan (Af) loved pet
Pacifica (L) peaceful
Padma (Sa) lotus
Pagan (L) heathen
✱ **Page** (F) attendant. Paige
Paka (Af) little kitten
Palila (Ha) bird
Pallas (Gk) goddess
Palma (L) palm tree. Palmira
Paloma (S) dove
Pamela (Gk) loving
Pandita (Sa) scholar
Pandora (Gk) gifted
Pansy (E) from the name of
  the flower
Panya (Af) little mouse
Paradise heaven
Pare Maori form of **Polly**
Paris from the name of the
  city in France
Parnella (F) little rock.
  Parnelle
Parthenia (Gk) maiden
Parvati (Sa) from the
  mountain

43

Pascale (F) Easter.
Pascaline Pascuala Pashal
Pasquelina Pasquette
Patience (E) patience
Patricia (L) noble. Paddy Pat
Patrice Patsy Patty Tricia
Trish Trisha
Paula (L) small. Paola
Pauletta Paulette Paulina
Pauline
Pax (Gk) peace. Paz
Peace (E) peace
Peaches from the name of
the fruit
Pearl (E) pearl
Peg, **Peggy** see **Margaret**
Pelagia (Gk) of the sea,
mermaid
Penelope (Gk) weaver. Penny
Penina (H) coral
Peony (Gk) from the name of
the flower. Paeony
Pepper (E) from the name of
the spice
Perdita (L) lost
Perfecta (L) perfect
Perpetua (L) continuing
Perrine (F) one who lives by
the pear tree. Perri Perrin
Perry
Persis (Gk) Persian woman

Peta (Gk) female form of
Peter
Petra (Gk) stone. Petronella
Petronilla Pier Pieta
Petula (E) from the name of
the flowers petunia and
tulip
Petunia (L) from the name of
the flower
Phedra (Gk) bright. Phaedra
Phila (Gk) loving
Philana (Gk) friend of
humanity
Philantha (Gk) lover of
flowers
Philberta (E) brilliant.
Filberta
Philippa (Gk) lover of horses.
Phillippa Pip Pippa
Phillida see **Phyllis**
Philomela (Gk) lover of song
Philomena (Gk) I am loved
Phoebe (Gk) the shining one.
Phebe
Phyllis (Gk) leafy. Phil
Phillida Phillis Phyllida
Pia (I) devout
Piala (Ir) prudent
Pier, **Pieta** see **Petra**
Pilar (S) pillar
Pina (S) pine tree

Piper (E) pipe player
Pippa Italian form of **Philippa**
Pixie (E) from the name of the elf
Polly see **Mary**
Polydora (Gk) gifts
Pomona (L) fruitful
Poppy (E) from the name of the flower
Portia (L) offering
Posy (E) a bunch of flowers. Posey
Prairie desert
Prema (Sa) love
Prima (L) first child
Primavera (I) spring (the season)
Primrose (E) from the name of the flower
Primula (L) from the name of the flower
Priscilla (L) of ancient lineage. Cilla
Priya (Sa) beloved
Prospera (L) favourable
Prudence (E) discretion. Pru Prue
Prunella (F) plum. Pru Prue
Psyche (Gk) soul
Pua (Ha) flower

Punita (Sa) pure
Pura (L) pure, purity

Qadira (A) powerful. Kadira
Qamra (A) moon. Kamra
Qing (Ch) blue
Qitura (A) fragrant
Queenie (OE) queen. Kuini Queena Quinn
Quenby (Sc) feminine
Quentin (L) fifth child. Quinta Quintan Quintana
Querida (S) beloved. Cherida
Questa (F) quest, search
Quinn (Ir) from the surname O'Quinn
Quinta (L) fifth child. Quintilla
Quintessa (L) essence. Quentessa
Quita (F) tranquil

45

NAMES OF FAMOUS WRITERS

Boys

Albert Camus
Bryce Courtenay
Charles Dickens
Dylan Thomas
Edgar Allan Poe
Ernest Hemingway
George Orwell
Henry James
Ian McEwan
James Joyce
Leo Tolstoy
Lewis Carroll
Louis de Bernieres
Mark Twain
Oscar Wilde
Peter Carey
Roald Dahl
Samuel Beckett
Stephen King
Tim Winton
Walt Whitman

Girls

Agatha Christie
Anita Brookner
Ann Patchett
Beryl Bainbridge
Carol Shields
Charlotte Bronte
Doris Lessing
Emily Bronte
Enid Blyton
Flannery O'Connor
Germaine Greer
Helen Garner
Iris Murdoch
Jane Austen
Janet Frame
Margaret Atwood
Maxine Hong Kingston
Olivia Goldsmith
Simone de Beauvoir
Virginia Wolf
Zadie Smith

R

Rabia (A) fragrant garden. Rabi

Rachel (H) ewe. Rachael Rachelle Rae Raquel Shelley

Rachida (A) wise

Rada (Sl) glad. Radinka

Radcliffe (E) red cliffs

Radha (Sa) success

Radinka (Sl) one who does good work

Radmilla (Sl) worker for the people

Rae (OE) doe. See **Rachel**

Raelene (Au) Raeline

Raewyn combination of **Rae** and **Wynne**

Ragini (Sa) melody

Rahima (A) compassionate. Raheema

Raine (F) regal. Raina Raine Rane Rayna Rayne Reine Reinette Reyna

Raja (Sa) hope

Rajani (Sa) of the night

Ramona (T) mighty protector

Rana (Sa) queen. Ranee Rani

Rane (Sc) pure

Rangi (M) sky

Rani (Sa) queen. Rajni Rania

Rapa (Ha) moonbeam

Raphaela (H) God has healed. Rafaela

Raquel Spanish form of **Rachel**

Rashida (A) righteous

Rasia (Gk) rose. Rasine

Rata (M) friendly

Raven from the name of the bird

Raya (H) friend

Rayna (H) clean and pure

Rea (Gk) poppy (the flower)

Reba see **Rebecca**

Rebecca (H) heifer. Becca Becky Reba Rebakah Ripeka

Reece (W) female form of Rhys, impetuous

Reena (Gk) peaceful

Regan (Ir) noble

Regine (L) queen. Gina Regina

Remi (F) woman from Reims in France. Remy

Rena (Gk) peace
Renata (L) born again.
   Renate Renee
Renee (F) reborn. Renata
Reseda (S) fragrant blossom
Reyna (Gk) peaceful. Reyne
Rhea (Gk) mother of the
   gods
Rhiannon (W) nymph.
   Rhiamon Rhianon
Rhoda (Gk) rose
Rhonda (W) grand. Rhondda
Rhonwen (W) lance. Rhona
Ria (S) river
Riana Maori form of **Diana**
Richenda (T) ruler. Richarda
   Richenza
Rida (A) favoured by God
Riley (Ga) valiant
Rimona (H) pomegranate
Rina (Sa) queen, regal
Ripeka Maori form of
   Rebecca
Rita see **Margaret**
Riva (F) river
Roberta (T) bright fame.
   Robin Robina Robyn
Robin, **Robyn** see **Roberta**
Rochelle (L) little rock.
   Rochella
Rocio (S) dew

Rodi (Gk) pomegranate
Roma (L) from the name of
   the city
Romaine (F) a woman from
   Rome. Romana Romola
Romola (L) woman of Rome
Rona (Ga) seal. Rhona
Ronnie see **Veronica**
Rory (Ir) red. Rori
Rosa Italian form of **Rose**
Rosalba (L) white rose
Rosalie see **Rose**
Rosalind (T) beautiful rose
Rosamond (L) pure rose. Ros
   Rosamund
Rosanna see **Rose**
Rosario (S) rosary. Rosaria
Rose (E) from the name of
   the flower. Rosa Rosalie
   Rosanna Rosetta Rosie
   Rosina Rosita
Rosemary combination of
   Rose and **Mary**
Rouge (F) red
Rowena (OE) famous friend
Roxana (P) dawn. Roxanna
   Roxanne Roxie Roxy
Rubena (H) behold, my
   daughter. Reubena
   Reubina Rubina Rubine

Ruby (E) from the name of
the jewel

Ruha, **Ruihi** Maori form of
Lucy

Ruiha Maori form of **Louisa**

Rumer (E) gypsy. Ruma

Ruth (H) friend. Rutu

Rutu Maori form of **Ruth**

Saba (A) sabah

Sabi (A) young one

Sabia (Ir) sweet

Sabina (L) Sabine woman.
Sabin

Sabira (A) patient

Sable (E) dark. Sabela
Sabelle

Sabra (H) restful

Sabrina (L) goddess of the
River Severn. Sabre

Sacha Russian form of
Alexandra

Sadie see **Sarah**

Saffron from the name of
the plant

Safiya (Af) pure

Sage (L) from the name of
the plant

Sahara (A) from the name of
the desert

Sakari (NA) sweet

Salah (A) goodness

Salima (A) peaceful. Salama
Salema Salma Selima

Salina (F) of the sea. Salena

Sally see **Sarah**

Salome (H) peaceful

Salvadora (S) saviour

Samantha (H) listener. Sam
Sammy

Samara (H) guarded by God

Saminah (A) sincere.
Sameema

Samira (A) evening
entertainer. Sameera

Sanchia (S) sacred,
sanctified. Sancha Sancia

Sandra Italian form of
Alexandra

Sanura (Af) clever, creative

Sapphire (Gk) eyes of
sapphire blue

Sarah (H) princess. Hera
Sadie Sally Sara Shari
Zara

Sarasa (Sa) beautiful

49

Sasha Russian form of **Alexandra**

Savannah (S) from the name of the open grasslands

Scarlett (E) red

Scout to observe, to explore

Sean (Ir) feminine form of John. Shawn

Sebastiane (L) venerable. Sebastiana

Sela (H) rock

Selda (E) rare. Zelda

Selina (F) heavenly. Celene Celie Celina Celine Selena Selene Seline

Selma (T) divinely protected. Anselma

Semele (Gk) the only one

Septima (L) seventh

Seraphina (H) burning. Serafina Serafine Seraphine

Serena (L) tranquil

Serenity calm, tranquil

Severine (F) stern. Severina

Shaina (H) beautiful

Shakila (A) pretty. Shaquilla

Shakira (A) grateful

Shandra modern version of **Sandra**

Shani (Af) wonderful

Shannon (C) slow waters

Shanti (Sa) peace. Santi

Shari Hungarian form of **Sarah**

Sharik (Af) gift from God

Sharmaine see **Charmaine**

Sharon (H) the plain. Sharron

Shasta (NA) the name of a mountain range in California

Shauna (Ir) female form of Shaun (Sean/John)

Shawn see **Sean**

Shayleen female form of Shay

Shea (Ir) palace or home of the fairies

Sheba (H) from Sheba. Saba

Sheena, **Shena** Gaelic forms of **Jane**

Sheila Irish form of **Cecilia**

Shelby (E) surname meaning 'a willow grove'

Shelley (OE) from the edge of the meadow. See also **Rachel**, **Sheila**

Sheridan (Ga) wild

Sherry see **Charlotte**, **Shirley**

Sheryl see **Cheryl**, **Shirley**

Shira (H) song
Shirley (OE) from the shining meadow. Sherry Sheryl
Shona Celtic form of **Jane**
Shoshannah (H) a lily, a rose
Shula (A) flaming
Shulamit (H) peaceful. Shulamith
Sibyl (Gk) prophet. Cybil Cybill Sybil
Sidra (L) star. Sidria
Sierra (S) from the Sierra mountain range
Sigourney (N) conqueror
Sigrid (N) victory ride
Silver (E) from the name of the metal. Silva
Silvestra (L) from the woods. Sylvestra
Silvia see **Sylvia**
Simka (H) rejoice
Simone (H) one who listens
Sine, **Sinead**, **Siobhan** Irish forms of **Jane**
Sirena (Gk) sweet singer
Sisi (Sa) ground furrow. Seeta
Sissy see **Cecilia**
Skye (Sc) an island off the coast of Scotland, the sky above. Sky

Slanie (Ir) health
Solana (S) sunshine. Soledad Solina Solita
Solange (F) solemn
Sonia Russian form of **Sophie**
Sophie (Gk) wisdom. Sofia Sofie Sonia Sonja Sonya Sophia Sophy
Sorcha (Ir) bright
Souline (F) dignified. Soule Zeline
Spencer (F) dispenser
Speranza (L) hope
Spring (E) springtime
Stacy see **Anastasia**
Stavroula (Gk) victorious, crown. Voola Voula
Stella (L) star
Stephanie (Gk) crowned. Stefanie Steffi Steffie Stephenie
Stevie female form of Steven
Stockard (E)
Storm (E) turbulent
Stormy (E) inclement weather
Suara (Sa) one who loves the sun
Suela (S) consolation. Consuela Suelita

Sula (Sc) sun
Sulia (L) young
Summer (E) summer
Sunita (Sa) conducted
Sunny (E) bright, cheerful. Sunshine
Susan (H) lily. Huhana Sue Sukey Suki Susanna Susannah Susie Suzanna Suzanne Suzette Suzie Zsa-Zsa
Sybil see **Sibyl**
Sydney from St Denis. Sidney Sidony
Sylvia (L) from the woods or forest. Silvaine Silvana Silvia Silvie Sylvan Sylvania Sylvette Sylvie

Tabina (A) one who follows Muhammad
Tabitha (H) gazelle
Tacy (L) be peaceful. Tace Tacey
Tahira (A) pure

Tahlia (H) fresh as the morning. Talor
Taite (E) cheerful. Tait
Taja (A) crown, coronet
Takia (A) to worship
Tale (Af) the colour green
Talia (Gk) blooming. Tali Talya
Talitha (A) graceful as a gazelle
Tallis (F) of the forest. Tallys
Tallulah (NA) leaping water
Tamara (H) palm tree. Tammy
Tamesis (Gk) goddess of the river
Tamma (H) perfect
Tamsin Cornish form of **Thomasin**
Tania, **Tanya** pet form of **Tatiana**
Tansy (L) tenacious
Tao (Ch) peach
Tara (Ga) from the rocky pinnacle
Tarana (Af) one born during the day
Tarati Maori form of **Dorothy**
Taryn see **Karen**

Tatiana (R) meaning unknown. Tania Tanya
Tatum (OE) cheerful. Tate
Taura (L) bull
Tavia (E) great one
Tawny (F) tanned
Taylor (OE) tailor
Tea (S) princess. Tia Tiana
Tegan (W) beautiful
Tegwen (W) pretty
Telma (Gk) ambitious
Temina (H) honest. Temima
Tempe (Gk) beautiful
Temperence (L) the virtue of moderation and sobriety
Tempest (E) stormy
Terehia Maori form of **Teresa**
Teresa (Gk) harvester. Terehia Terese Teri Terry Tess Tessa Tessie Theresa Therese Tracey Tracy
Terra (L) earth. Terena
Terry see **Teresa**
Tess see **Teresa**
Tessa (Gk) fourth child. See also **Teresa**
Thaddea (Gk) courageous. Thadda Thadine
Thalassa (Gk) from the sea
Thalia (Gk) blooming. Talia

Thana (A) gratitude
Thandie (A) beloved. Tandi
Thara (A) wealthy
Thea (Gk) goddess. See also **Althea**
Thelma (Gk) nursling
Thema (Af) queen, regal
Theodora (Gk) gift of God. Dora Fedora Feodora Teddie Theo Theodosia
Theola (Gk) divine. Theone
Theophania (Gk) manifestation of God. Tiffany Tiffeny
Theore (Gk) thinker. Theoris
Thera (Gk) wild
Theresa, **Therese** see **Teresa**
Thina (Gk) wise
Thirza (H) pleasant
Thomasin (H) twin. Tamasine Tammy Tamsin Thomasina Thomasine Tommie
Thora (Sc) thunder
Tiana (Gk) princess
Tiara (L) from the name of the crown
Tiaret (Af) lioness
Tierney (Ir) descendant of a lord
Tieve (Ir) from the hillside

Tiffany English form of
Theophania

Tiger from the name of the
animal

Tigris (Ir) a sister of St
Patrick

Tina see **Christina**, **Martine**

Ting (Ch) tall, slim, graceful

Tira (H) enclosure. Tirra

Tirion (W) gentle

Titania (Gk) giant one

Tivona (H) one who loves
nature. Tibona

Tobie (H) God is good. Toba
Tobia Tobsha

Toni see **Antonia**

Tova (H) good. Tovah Tove

Toyah (E) one with whims

Trace (E) brave

Tracy (Ga) battler. Tracey.
See also **Teresa**

Treasa (Ir) strength

Treasure (Gk) hidden riches

Tricia, **Trisha** see **Patricia**

Trina (Gk) pure

Trinity (L) trio. Trini Trinie

Trista (L) melancholy.
Tristana Tristessa Tristesse

Trixie see **Beatrice**

Trixiebelle combination of
Trixie and **Belle**

Trudy (T) beloved. Trudie.
See also **Gertrude**

Tryphena (Gk) dainty.
Tryphosa

Tuesday (E) from the day of
the week

Tui (M) from the name of
the bird

Tulia (S) glorious

Tullia (Ir) peaceful. Tully

Turuhira Maori form of
Judith

Tybal (E) holy place

Tyler (OE) tile maker

Tyra (Sc) battler. Tyronica

Udele (E) prosperous. Uda
Udelia Udella Udelle

Ula (C) sea jewel

Ulani (Ha) cheerful

Ulema (A) wise. Ulima

Ulla (E) to fill, will

Ulma (L) from the elm tree

Ulrica (T) wolf ruler. Ulrika

Ultima (L) ultimate, greatest

Ulva (N) she-wolf
Uma (Sa) light, peace
Una (L) one. Oona Oonagh
Undine (L) of the sea. Ondine Undina
Undrine (L) water sprite. Ondrine
Unity (E) unity
Urania (Gk) heavenly
Urbana (L) urban
Ursula (L) little she-bear. Ursa Ursuline
Usha (Sa) of the dawn
Utopia (Gk) good
Utsa (Sa) spring (the season)

Valda (T) inspiration in battle
Vale (F) lives in the valley. Vail
Valentina (L) strong, healthy. Val Valentine
Valerie (L) brave. Val Valeria Valora
Valeska (Sl) great leader
Valmai (W) mayflower

Vanessa (Gk) butterfly. Nessa Vania
Vania, Vanya Russian forms of **Jane**
Varda (A) rose. Vardis
Veda (Sa) wise
Vedette (F) actor. Vedetta
Vega (A) falling star
Velma see **Wilhelmina**
Velvet (E) velvety
Venetia see **Gwyneth**, **Venus**
Ventura (S) fortune, luck
Venus (L) goddess of love. Venetia Venice Venita
Vera (R) faith. See also **Veronica**
Verda (L) young, fresh
Verena (T) defender
Verity (E) truth
Verna (L) spring-like. See also **Laverne**
Veronica (L) true image. Ronnie Vera Verona Vonnie
Vespera (Gk) evening
Vesta (L) goddess of fire
Victoria (L) victory. Vicky Vita Vittoria
Vida (H) beloved
Vidula (Sa) moon
Vila (L) country house. Villa

55

CHARACTERS FOUND IN FICTION AND FILM

Boys

Atticus (Finch): Harper Lee's novel *To Kill a Mockingbird*
Bertie (Wooster): P.G. Wodehouse's Jeeves novels
Charlie (Brown): The comic book series *Peanuts*
Clark (Kent): The comic book series *Superman*
Darcy (Mr): Jane Austen's novel *Pride and Prejudice*
Don (Quixote): Miguel Cervantes's novel *Don Quixote*
Forrest (Gump): The movie *Forrest Gump*
Harry (Potter): J.K. Rowling's Harry Potter books
Heathcliff: Emily Bronte's novel *Wuthering Heights*
Holden (Caulfield): J. D. Salinger's novel
The Catcher in the Rye
Hunter: The movie *Paris, Texas*
James (Bond): Ian Fleming's James Bond novels
Jay (Gatsby): F. Scott Fitzgerald's novel *The Great Gatsby*
Lenny: John Steinbeck's novel *The Grapes of Wrath*
Leopold (Bloom): James Joyce's novel *Ulysses*
Robin (Hood): Howard Pyle's book *The Adventures of Robin Hood*
Romeo (Montague): Shakespeare's play *Romeo and Juliet*
Sam (Spade): Dashiell Hammett's novel
The Maltese Falcon
Tom (Sawyer): Mark Twain's novel *The Adventures of Tom Sawyer*
Travis (Bickle): The film *Taxi Driver*

Girls

Alice: Lewis Carroll's book *Alice in Wonderland*
Annie: Woody Allen's film *Annie Hall*
Bridget (Jones): Helen Fielding's novel *Bridget Jones's Diary*
Charlotte: E. B. White's book *Charlotte's Web*
Clarissa (Dalloway): Virginia Wolf's novel *Mrs Dalloway*
Dorothy (Gale): The film *The Wizard of Oz*
Elizabeth (Bennet): Jane Austen's novel *Pride and Prejudice*
Hermoine (Grainger): J. K. Rowling's Harry Potter books
Holly (Golightly): Truman Capote's novel *Breakfast at Tiffany's*
Imogen: Shakespeare's play *Cynneline*
Juliet (Capulet): Shakespeare's play *Romeo and Juliet*
Lara: Boris Pasternak's novel *Dr Zhivago*
Lois (Lane): The comic book series *Superman*
Margo (Charming): The film *All About Eve*
Mary (Poppins): P. L. Travers's book *Mary Poppins*
Norma (Desmond): The film *Sunset Boulevard*
Ophelia: Shakespeare's play *Hamlet*
Penelope: Homer's epic poem *Odyssey*
Scarlett (O'Hara): Margaret Mitchell's novel *Gone with the Wind*
Wendy (Darling): J. M. Barrie's story *Peter Pan*

Villette (F) small town

Vina (S) of the vineyard. Vinna Vinnia

Vincentia (L) conqueror. Vincenza

Violet (F) from the name of the flower. Iolande Iolanthe Vi Viola Violante Violetta Violette Yolanda Yolande

Virginia (L) from the Roman family Verginius. Ginger Ginny Virginie

Vita (L) full of life. See also **Victoria**

Vivien (L) alive. Viv Viviana Vivianne Vivienne Vyvyan

Volante (I) to fly

Vonnie see **Veronica**, **Yvonne**

Walida (A) newborn girl

Wallis (OE) from Wales

Wanda (T) shepherd. Wendy

Wanetta (E) pale, fair. Wanette

Wednesday (E) Woden's day

Wendy see **Gwendolyn**. Wanda Wenda

Whitney (OE) from the white island

Wilhelmina (T) resolute protector. Billie Velma Willa Willie Wilma

Willow (E) willow tree

Wilma see **Wilhelmina**

Wilona (E) desired

Winifred (W) friend of peace. Freda Win Winnie

Winnie see **Gwyneth**, **Winifred**

Winona (NA) first born. Wenona Wenonah

Winsome (E) pleasantly attractive

Wyetta female form of Wyatt

Wynelle (E) fair, blessed

Wynne (C) fair

Xanthe (Gk) golden-haired

Xanthippe (Gk) yellow horse
Xaviera (A) bright
Xena (Gk) hospitable. Xenia
  Zena
Xiaoli (Ch) small, pretty
Ximena (Gk) Heroine
Xylia (Gk) from the woods
Xylona (Gk) one who loves
  woods, forests and trees.
  Xyla Xylina Xylophila

Yetta (OE) giver
Yolanda, **Yolande** French
  forms of **Violet**
Yonina (H) dove. Jonina Yona
  Yonine Yonita
Yoorana (Au) loving
Ysabel French form of
  Elizabeth
Yu (Ch) jade
Yvonne (T) yew tree. Evonne
  Vonnie Yvette

Yael (H) wild goat. Jael Yaelle
Yaffa (H) beautiful. Yaffah
Yakira (H) precious
Yang (Ch) sun
Yashoda (Sa) one who gives
  success
Yasmin Persian form of
  Jasmin
Yedda (E) one with a
  melodious voice
Yeira (H) light
Yemina (H) dove
Yen (Ch) pretty
Yesenia (A) flower

Zada (A) lucky. Zadah Zaida
  Zaidee
Zafira (A) successful. Zafirah
Zahara (Af) flower
Zahava (H) golden one.
  Zahavah
Zainab (A) the prophet's
  daughter. Zianabu
Zakia (A) chaste
Zalika (A) well-born
Zamira (H) song
Zandra see **Alexandra**

Zaneta (H) grace of God.
  Zanetta
Zara (H) sunrise. See also
  Sarah
Zariza (H) industrious
Zehava (H) gold. Zehavi
Zehira (H) protected
Zelda see **Griselda**
Zelene (E) sunshine. Zelia
Zelia (Gk) zealous. Zelie
Zemira (Gk) song of joy
Zena see **Xena**
Zephira (H) morning
Zephyr (Gk) west wind.
  Zephrine Zephyrine
Zerlinda (H) beautiful as the
  dawn
Zeta (H) olive. Zetta
Zeva (Gk) sword
Zevida (H) gift
Zia (L) grain. Zea
Zibia (H) shade. Zila Zilah
  Zillah
Zillah (H) shade. Zilla
Zina (Af) name
Zippora (H) bird
Zissa (H) sweet
Zita (F) bedroom
Zoe (Gk) life
Zola (I) ball of earth
Zorina (Sl) golden. Zorana

Zsa-Zsa Hungarian form of
  Susan
Zuleika (A) fair
Zulema (A) peace. Suleima
  Zulima
Zuriel (H) God is my rock

Boys

Aaron (H) high mountain. Aron

Aba (H) father

Abbott (OE) head of the abbey. Abbot Abby

Abdiel (H) servant of God

Abdul (A) son

Abel (H) breath

Abelard (Gk) noble

Abi (H) great. Abia

Abiel (H) God is my father

Abijah (H) God is my father

Abner (H) father of light. Avner Evner

Abraham (H) father of a multitude. Abe Abram Aperahama Avram Bram

Absolom (H) the divine father is peace

Acacio (H) God holds him

Ace (L) unit, one

Acelin (F) noble

Ackerley (E) dweller in the meadow. Ackley

Acton (H) from a village with oak trees

Adair (Ga) from the oak tree ford

Adam (H) red-skinned. Addy Arama Atama

Adar (H) chaste. Adara

Addison (OE) son of Adam

Adeeb (A) scholarly. Adib

Adelpho (Gk) brother

Aden (H) handsome one. Aidan

Adil (A) just

Adin (H) pleasant

Adlai (H) my witness

Adler (T) eagle

Admon (H) healthy, ruddy

Adney (E) from the noble person's island

61

Adolphus (T) noble wolf.
Adolf Adolph Adolphe
Adolpho

Adrian (L) from the Adriatic.
Ade Adriano Adrien
Hadrian

Aeneas (Gk) worthy of praise

Aeron (W) berry

Afonso (S) noble, battle
ready

Agatone (Gk) good

Agostino (I) celebrated

Ahab (H) uncle

Ahearn (Ir) owner of horses.
Aherin Ahern Aherne

Ahmed (A) highly praised.
Ahmad

Aidan (Ga) fiery

Aiken (E) little Adam. Aickin
Aikin

Aimery (E) home ruler

Aimon (F) to love

Ainslie (Ga) from one's own
meadow. Ainsley

Ajax (Gk) from the earth.
Eagle

Ajay (Sa) invincible

Akram (A) generous, noble

Aladdin (A) servant of Allah

Alaire (F) joyous

Alan (C) harmony. Alain
Allan Allen

Aland (E) bright as the sun

Alaric (T) ruler of all

Alastair Scottish form of
Alexander

Alban (L) fair. Alben

Albern (E) noble warrior

Albert (T) noble, illustrious.
Albie Arapata Bert

Albion (L) white, blond

Alcott (E) cottage dweller

Alden (OE) old, wise friend.
Elden Eldon

Aldous (T) old, wise. Aldo
Aldus

Aldred (E) great counsellor.
Eldred

Aldrich (E) old, wise ruler.
Aldric Audrich Eldric
Eldrich

Alec see **Alexander**

Aled (W) offspring

Aleron (F) knight

Alexander (Gk) defender of
men. Al Alasdair Alastair
Alec Alessandro Alex
Alic Alick Alistair Alister
Araketenara Arekahanara
Sacha Sandy

Alexis (Gk) defender

Alfio (I) white
Alfred (OE) elf counsellor.
  Alfie Arapeti Avery Fred
  Freddy
Algernon (F) bearded one
Ali (A) exalted
Alijah (H) Lord is my god
Alistair Scottish form of
  Alexander
Allan see **Alan**
Allard (OE) noble, brave
Almo (E) noble, famous
Alon (H) oak
Aloysius see **Lewis**
Alphonse (T) ready, eager.
  Alf Alfonso Alfonzo Alonso
  Alonzo Alphonso Fonz
  Fonzie
Alroy (Ir) red-haired boy
Alston (E) from the
  nobleman's settlement
Altair (A) star. Altaira
Alton (T) from the old town.
  Alten
Alvah (H) exalted one
Alvaro (S) cautious
Alvin (T) friend of all. Alwin
  Elvin
Amadeus (I) lover of God.
  Amadeo Amado
Amador (S) lover. Amato

Amal (A) hope
Amar (Sa) immortal
Amarus (Gk) endless love
Amato (S) beloved
Ambrose (Gk) immortal.
  Ambros Emrys
Amiel (H) of the people
Amin (A) trustworthy
Amir (A) princely
Amirov (H) my people are
  great
Amistad (S) friendship
Amitav (Sa) endless
  splendour. Amit Amitabh
Amoho Maori form of **Amos**
Amon (H) hidden
Amory (T) famous ruler.
  Amery Emery
Amos (H) carried. Amoho
An (Ch) peace
Analu (Ha) manly
Anand (Sa) joy
Anando (Af) bliss. Anand
Anaru Maori form of
  Andrew
Anastasios (Gk) resurrection.
  Anastase Anastasius
Anatole (Gk) from the east
Ancel (T) a god. Ansel
Anders Swedish form of
  Andrew

Andre French form of
Andrew

Andrew (Gk) manly. Anaru
Anders Andre Andreas
Andy Drew

Anestes (Gk) one who has
risen

Aneurin (W) famous. Aneirin
Nye

Angelo (Gk) messenger.
Angel Angell

Angus (Ga) outstanding.
Ennis

Anian (W) personality

Anil (Sa) air

Anoki (NA) actor. Anoke

Ansel (F) follows nobility.
Ansell

Anselem (T) divine helmet.
Ancelm Elmo

Ansley (OE) from Ann's
meadow

Anson (OE) Ann's son

Anthony (L) priceless.
Antoine Anton Antonio
Antony Atonio Tonio Tony

Anwar (Af) brightest one

Aperahama Maori form of
Abraham

Apollo (Gk) beautiful boy.
Apollonas

Aquila (S) eagle

Ara (H) pure

Araketenara Maori form of
Alexander

Arama Maori form of **Adam**

Aran (H) active

Arapata Maori form of
Albert

Arapeti Maori form of
Alfred

Archer (E) bowman

Archibald (T) genuinely bold.
Arch Archie

Ardal (Ir) valour

Arden (L) fervent

Argus (Gk) vigilant

Ari (H) lion. Ariel

Arial (W) strength

Aric (T) ruler

Ariel (H) lion of God

Aristedes (Gk) descended
from the best. Aristo

Arjun (Sa) diligent

Arlen (Ga) pledge

Arley (E) from the hare
or stag meadow. Arlie
Harleigh Harley Hartley

Arlo (S) barbary

Armand French form of
Herman

Armstrong (OE) strong arm

Arnold (T) powerful eagle.
Arnaud Arnie
Arrio (S) warlike, warrior
Arsenio (Gk) manly, virile
Artemus (Gk) from the moon
Arthur (C) bear. Art Arturo
Arun (Sa) morning sun
Arvad (H) wanderer
Arvin (T) friend of the people
Asa (H) healer
Asad (A) lion
Ashby (OE) from the ash
tree farm
Asher (H) blessed
Ashley (OE) from the ash
tree meadow
Ashling (E) dream
Ashton (E) ash tree,
settlement
Ashwin (Sa) star
Aston (OE) eastern town
Atherton (E) from the town
by the spring
Atley (E) from the meadow.
Atleigh
Atonio Maori form of
Anthony
Attila (Gk) little father.
Attilio
Auberon (F) noble. Auber
Oberon

Aubrey (T) elf ruler. Albery
Auberon Oberon
Augustus (L) venerable.
August Augustine Austin
Gus
Aurelius (L) golden one.
Aurel Aurele Aurelian
Aurelio Auryn
Austin see **Augustus**
Avan (H) proud
Avel (Gk) breath
Averill (OE) slayer of the
boar. Averil
Avery see **Alfred**
Avi (H) divine father
Aviv (H) spring (the season)
Avram see **Abraham**
Axel (T) father of peace
Aylwin (OE) noble friend.
Alwin
Azariah (H) God helps
Aziz (A) powerful one
Azriel (H) angel of God

Bachir (A) welcome

Badar (A) full moon. Badr Badur

Bade (E) to urge or encourage. Baide Bayde

Badhur (A) born at the full moon. Badhir

Baez (W) boar

Baha (A) splendour

Bahari (Af) boy or man of the sea

Bailey (F) steward. Baily Bayley

Bain (Ir) fair-haired. Baine Bayne

Baird (Ga) minstrel. Bard

Bais (A) awake

Bal (Sa) child with much hair

Baldasarre (I) brave

Baldev (Sa) God of strength

Baldric (E) bold. Baldrick Baldryck Baudrey

Baldwin (T) bold protector

Balfour (Ga) pasture land

Bancroft (OE) from the bean field

Bane (Ha) long-awaited child. Baine Bayne

Bannock (R) one who has been exiled

Banquo (Ga) fair, white

Banyan (E) banyan tree

Bao (Ch) treasure

Baptiste (F) to dip. Batista Battista Bautista

Barak (A) lightning

Barclay (E) from the birch tree meadow. Berkeley Berkley

Bardolf (E) fierce wolf

Barker (E) shepherd

Barley (E) of the barley farm. Barton Beretun Berford

Barlow (E) from the bare hill. Barlowe

Barnabas (H) son of consolation. Barnaby Barney

Barnard see **Bernard**

Barnes (E) from the barns. Barney

Barnum (E) from the barn

Baron (E) son of Aaron. Barren Barron

Barrett (T) mighty as a bear. Barret

Barrington (E) from the fenced town

Barris (Ga) Barry's son

Barry (Ga) spear. Barrie

Bartholomew (H) son of the farmer. Bart Barth

Barto (S) from the hill

Barton (OE) barley farmer. ·Bart

Bartram see **Bertram**

Baruch (H) blessed

Basam (A) smiling. Basem Basim Bassam Bassem Bassim

Baseer (A) intelligent

✱**Basil** (Gk) kingly

Batiste (F) fine cloth

Baurice modern version of **Maurice**

Baxter (OE) baker

Bay (L) with brown hair. Bayard Bayarde Bayhard

Bayard (OE) having red-brown hair

Beagan (Ir) little one

Beattie (Ir) provider of gladness, blessings and joy

Beau (F) handsome

Beaufort (F) handsome

Beaumont (F) handsome hill or mountain

Beauregard (F) beautiful expression

Becan (Ir) little one

Bechor (H) first born

Beck (Sc) brook

Bede (E) prayer

Bedros (Gk) stone

Belden (F) from the beautiful valley. Beldon

Belen (Gk) arrow

Bellamy (F) handsome friend

Belveder (I) beautiful. Belvedere Belvidere Belvydere

Ben (H) son. Benny

Benedict (L) blessed. Ben Benedick Benito Benney Benny

Benito (I) blessed. Benedo Benino Bennito Benyto

Benjamin (H) son of the right hand. Ben Benjy Benny

Bennett (L) blessed

Benson (H) son of Benjamin

Bentley (E) from the meadow

Benton (E) where bent grass grows

Berenger (F) strength of a bear

Bergen (Sc) lives on the hill. Bergin Birgin

Berkeley (E) from the birch woods. Barclay Berkley

Bernard (T) as brave as a bear. Barnard Barnett Barney Bernhard Bernie

Bert see **Albert**, **Bertram**, **Herbert**, **Lambert**

Bertram (T) bright raven. Bartram Bert Bertie Bertrand

Berwick (T) barley field

Bevan (W) young archer.

Bevis (Ga) from the plain

Bharat (Sa) seeker of knowledge

Bhaskar (Sc) shining light

Bhina (Sa) mighty one

Birch (E) from a grove of birch trees

Birchall (OE) dweller near the birch trees

Bishop (E) bishop (the clerical title)

Blade (E) fame, prosperity

Blain (Ir) thin, lean. Blaine Blane Blayne

Blaise (L) stammerer. Blasé Blaze

Blake (OE) fair

Blaxland (E) from the black lands

Bob, **Bobby** see **Robert**

Bogart (F) strong bow

Bogdan (Sl) gift from God. Bohdan

Bolton (E) from the manor farm

Bonar (F) kind, gentle. Bonnar Bonner

Bonaventure (I) good luck

Bond (E) tiller of the soil

Boneton (OE) from the moor

Bonifacio (I) good fate

Booker (E) written document. Beech

Boone (F) good

Booth (OE) from the hut. Boothe

Borg (Sc) one who lives in a castle

Boris (Sl) warrior

Bosley (E) from a grove of trees

Boston from the place name

Bowen (Ga) yellow-haired. Bowie

Boyce (F) from the wood

Boyd (Ir) light-haired

Brac (W) free

Braden (OE) from the wide valley

Bradford (E) broad crossing, broad stream

Bradley (OE) from the broad meadow. Brad

Brady (Ga) from the broad island

Bramwell (Ir) well near the bramble bush

Brandon (OE) beacon on the hill. Braydon

Brannon (Ga) son of Bran

Branton (OE) dweller by the brushwood hill

Braydon see **Brandon**

Brendan (Ga) little raven. Brenden Brendon Brennan Bryn

Brent (OE) steep hill

Brett (C) from Brittany. Bret

Brewster (OE) brewer. Brewer

Brian (Ga) strength. Brien Bryan

Brice (C) swift, ambitious. Bryce

Bridon modern name, derivation unknown

Brigham (E) from the house by the bridge

Brighton (E) British. Bryton

Britt (H) helpful

Brock (OE) badger

Broderick (E) son of the ruler. Roderick

Brody (E) black

Bromley (E) from where the broom grows

Brone (E) brown-haired

Bronislav (Sl) glorious weapon. Bronislaw

Bronson (OE) son of the brown-haired one

Brook (E) surname meaning 'a stream'. Brooke Brooklyn

Brooklyn (E) see **Brook**

Bruce (F) from the thicket

Bruno (T) brown-haired

Brutus (L) heavy, stupid

Bryant (Ir) strong, reliable

Bryce (Ir) ambition. Brice

Bryden (Ga) strong

Bryn (W) hill. Brin Brynmor

Buck (OE) deer

Bud (OE) herald. Budd

Burgess (OE) from the fortified town

Burke (E) fort, manor. Berke Bourke

Burleigh (E) clearing with a fort or manor. Burley
Burton (E) stronghold
Butler (F) chief steward
Byron (F) from the cottage

Cable (E) rope maker. Cabel
Cachi (S) one who brings peace
Cade (E) cask, barrel
Cadman (W) soldier
Cadmus (Gk) man who excels
Cadoc (W) ready for battle. Caddock
Cadogan (W) battle honour
Cadwallader (W) battle leader
Caelen (Ir) powerful warrior. Cael Caelean Caelin Caylan Caylin
Caesar (L) emperor. Cesar
Cailan (Ir) child
Cain (H) spear. Caine Kane

Cairn (W) landmark, memorial of piled stones. Carne
Caius (L) rejoice. Cai Caio Caw
Calder (E) stream. Cal
Caldwell (OE) from the cold spring. Cal
Cale (Ga) thin, slender
Caleb (H) dog
Calis (Gk) handsome
Calisto (Gk) beautiful
Callum (Ga) named for St Columba. Calum
Calvert (OE) herdsman
Calvin (L) bald. Cal Vinnie
Cameron (Ga) crooked nose. Cam
Campbell (Ga) curved mouth. Cam
Cannon (F) church official. Cannan Canon
Canute (Sc) knot. Knute
Caolan (Ir) thin
Caradoc (W) amiable
Carel (F) strong
Carew (W) castle by the water
Carey (W) from near the castle. Cary
Carl German form of **Charles**

Carlin (Ga) little champion.
  Carling
Carlisle (E) from Carl's
  island. Carlyle
Carlos Greek form of
  Charles
Carlton (E) country farm
Carmichael (Ga) from St
  Michael's castle
Carmine (I) song. Carmelo
Carney (Ga) victorious
Caroll (Ir) champion warrior.
  Caryl
Carr (N) from the marsh.
  Kerr
Carson (OE) son of the
  marsh dweller
Carter (OE) cart driver
Carvel (F) one who lives in a
  swamp. Carvell
Carver (E) one who carves
Cary (E) honest and shy one.
  Carey
Case (Fr) dwelling place
Casey (Ga) brave
Casimir (Sl) bringer of peace.
  Kazimir Kazmer Kazek
  Kazik Kazio
Caspar German form of
  Jasper

Cassidy (Ir) ingenious, clever,
  trickster. Cass Cassady
Cassius (L) vain. Casius
Cathal (Ir) battle, rule
Cato (L) smart, wise
Catwallen (W) battle
  organiser. Cadwallon
Cavan (Ga) handsome. Kavan
Ceallachan (Ir) warrior.
  Cillan Cillian
Cecil (L) blind
Cedric (C) chieftain
Cemal (A) handsome
Cerdic (W) cherished.
  Ceredig
Cesare Kaiser
Chad (OE) warlike
Chago (S) heel. Chango
Chai (H) life
Chaim (H) life. Chaika
  Chaimek Hyam Khaim
Chal (E) boy
Chale (S) manly, powerful
Chalfon (H) change. Chalfan
  Halfan Halphon
Cham (H) hot
Chance (E) good fortune
Chand (Sa) shining moon.
  Chanda Chander
Chandler (F) candle maker

Chandrakant (Sa) loved by the moon
Chaney (F) oak tree. Cheney
Channing (F) canon
Chapman (OE) merchant
Charles (T) strong, manly. Carl Carlo Carlos Hare Karl Tiare
Charlton (OE) farmer's town
Charro (S) cowboy
Chase (F) hunter
Chasin (H) strong. Chason Hasin Hassin
Chata (Af) ending
Chauncey (F) record keeper. Chauncy
Ché (S) modern usage of Spanish nickname
Chen (Ch) vast, great
Chenche (S) conquer
Cheney (F) one from the forest
Cheng (Ch) accomplish, succeed
Chepe (H) God will multiply
Chester (L) from the fortified camp. Ches Chet
Chetwin (E) house on the winding path. Chet
Chevalier (F) knight. Cavalier
Chico (S) boy

Chilton (E) farm near a well
Chiram (H) worthy or exalted brother. Hirma
Chokichi (Ch) good luck
Chowdhury (A) landowner
Christian (L) a Christian. Chris Christy Kristian
Christopher (Gk) bearer of Christ. Chris Christophe Christos Cris Kester Kit Kristofer Kristos
Cian (Ir) ancient, in the past
Cianan (Ir) little Cian
Ciaran (Ir) with black hair. Ciardha
Cid (S) rooster, God
Ciel (F) from heaven
Ciro (S) French man
Clancy (Ir) ruddy warrior
Clarence (L) bright, famous
Clark (OE) learned man. Clarke
Claude (F) lame. Claud
Clay (OE) from the earth
Clayton (OE) from the town built on clay. Clay
Cleavon modern name, derivation unknown
Cledwyn (W) blessed sword
Clement (L) merciful. Clem
Cleon (Gk) famous

Cliff (OE) steep rock. See
also **Clifford**

Clifford (OE) from the ford
by the cliff. Cliff

Clifton (OE) from the town
by the cliff

Clinton (OE) from the farm
on the headland. Clint

Clive (OE) from the cliff.
Cleve Clyve

Cluny (Ga) the meadow

Clyde (W) warm

Cody (Ir) wealthy

Colbert (E) brilliant seafarer.
Colvert Culbert

Colby (Sc) from Kol's
settlement

Cole see **Coleman**, **Nicholas**

Coleman (OE) follower. Cole
Colman Nicholas

Colin (Ga) child. See also
Nicholas

Collier (OE) miner. Collis

Colum (Ga) dove. Colm

Coman (A) noble

Conal (C) high and mighty

Conan (C) high. Con

Cong (Ch) smart

Conlan (Ga) hero

Conn (C) high. Con

Connall (Ir) with the
strength of a wolf

Conor (Ir) high desire.
Connor

Conrad (T) bold counsellor.
Con Konrad Kurt

Conroy (Ir) wise man

Constant (L) constant

Constantine (L) firm,
constant. Constantin
Constantino Konstantin

Conway (Ga) hound of the
plain

Cooper (E) barrel maker

Coran (Ir) little moon

Corban (Gk) devoted to God

Corbet (E) dark as a raven.
Corbett Corbie Corbin
Cory

Corbin (F) raven

Cordelle (Fr) rope

Corey (Ga) from the hollow.
Corrie Cory

Cornelius (L) horned. Cornell

Corydon (Gk) lark (the bird)

Cosmo (Gk) beauty

Costa (Gk) stable, steady.
Kosta

Courtney (F) from the court.
Courtenay Courteney
Courtnay Curt

Couslon (E) triumphant. Colson

Cowan (Ga) hollow in the hillside

Coyne (F) modest

Craig (Ga) from the crag

Craven (E) cowardly

Crawford (E) ford of the crows

Cresswell (E) river with watercress

Crevan (Ir) fox

Crispin (L) curly-haired. Cris Crispian

Crosby (Sc) by the cross. Crosibe

Crossley modern usage of a surname

Crowther (E) fiddler

Cruz (S) one who bears the cross

Culver (E) dove. Colver

Curran (Ir) heroic

Curtis (F) courteous. Curt

Cuthbert (E) well-known, famous

Cynan (W) chief, leader. Kynan

Cyprian (Gk) from the island of Cyprus. Ciprian Cipriano Cyprien

Cyrano (Gk) from Cyrene

Cyril (Gk) lordly. Cyrill

Cyrus (P) the sun god

Dace (F) of nobility. Dayce

Dacey (Ir) from the south. Dacie Dacy Daicey Daicy

Daegan (Ir) dark-haired one. Daegen Daegon Daygon

Daemon (Gk) guiding spirit. Daemen

Dag (Sc) day. Dagmar

Dai (W) shine

Dakota (NA) allies

Dalbert (E) from the shining valley

Dale (OE) from the valley

Daley (Ir) assembly. Daly Dawley

Dallas (Ga) skilled, wise

Dalphin (F) dolphin

Dalton modern usage of a surname

Daly (Ga) counsellor. Daley

Damario (S) gentle. Demario

BOTANICAL NAMES

Boys	*Girls*
Alder	Blossom
Ashley	Camelia
Basil	Cherry
Bay	Dahlia
Birch	Daisy
Bruce	Fern
Burnet	Fleur
Eldridge	Ginger
Florian	Hazel
Forrest	Holly
Fraiser, Fraser	Iris
Garwood	Ivy
Grover	Jasmine
Harwood	Lavender
Heath	Lilac
Jarrah	Lily
Leaf, Leif	Magnolia
Linden	Olive
Lockwood	Pansy
Oakley	Poppy
Oliver	Posy
Perry	Rose
Silvanus	Saffrom
Stockton	Violet

Damek (Sl) man of the earth
Damian German form of
   Damon
Damocles (Gk) impending
   danger
Damon (Gk) constant.
   Damian Damien
Dana (T) from Denmark
Dandin (Sa) holy
Dane (E) from Denmark.
   Daine Dean
Daniel (H) God has judged.
   Dan Danny Raniera
Dante (L) enduring
Danyon (E) God is my judge.
   Danion
Darah (H) bold
Darby (Ir) free from envy.
   Derby
Darcy (F) from the fortress.
   D'Arcy
Darien (Gk) wealthy. Darian
   Dario
Dario see **Darius**
Darius (P) wealthy. Darien
   Dario
Darnell (F) hidden spot.
   Darnall Darnel
Darrell (F) beloved. Darrel
   Darryl Daryl
Darren (Ga) Darin Darrin

Darshan (Sa) holy vision
Darton (E) from the deer
   park
Darwin (T) courageous
Dashiell (F) page boy
David (H) darling. Dave
   Davey Davon Dewi Rawiri
   Rewi
Davin (Sc) shining
Davis (E) son of David.
   Davidson Davies Davison
   Dawson
Dawes (E) days
Dax (F) of the water
Daylon modern name,
   derivation unknown
Dayton (E) light town, day
   town
De (Ch) virtue
Deacon (E) church officer.
   Deakin
Dean (OE) from the valley.
   Deane Dino
Deangelo (I) from the
   angels. Dangelo
Decarlos (S) strong,
   courageous. Dacarlos
   Decarlo
Decimus (L) tenth
Declan (Ir) man of prayer.
   Decklan Deklan

Deepak (Sa) lamp. Dipak
Delaney (Ga) black, dark
Delano (F) of the night
Delbert (E) sunny day.
  Dalbert Dilbert
Dell (E) from the dell, valley
Delmar (S) from the sea.
  Delmer Delmor Delmore
  Elmer Elmore
Delon modern name,
  derivation unknown
Delroy (F) son of the king.
  Delroi Elroy Leroy
Delwin (E) proud friend.
  Dalwin Delavan Delevan
  Dellwin Delwyn Delwynn
  Delvin
Demas (Gk) popular
Demetrios (Gk) of
  agriculture and fertility
Demos (Gk) the people
Dempsey (Ir) proud one.
  Dempsy
Dempster (E) one who
  judges
Denbigh derived from the
  place name
Denby (Sc) by the valley.
  Danby Denbeigh
Denell modern name,
  derivation unknown

Denholm (OE) island in the
  valley
Denis (Gk) wine lover. Dennis
  Denny
Denley (E) from the meadow
Dennison (E) son of Dennis
Denton (E) town in the valley
Denver (E) from the edge of
  the green valley
Denzil (C) stronghold. Denzel
Derek (T) ruler of the people.
  Derreck Derrick Dirk
Dermot (C) free from envy.
  Diamit Diarmuit
Derwent (W) clear water
Deryn (W) bird. Derren
  Derryn
Desi (L) yearning. Dezi
Desmond (Ga) man from
  South Munster. Des
Destin (F) fate, destiny.
  Destan Desten
Dev (Sa) God-like. Deavan
  Deven
Devdan (Sa) gift of the gods
Deverell (W) from the river
  bank
Devin (Ga) poet. Devan
  Devon
Devlin (Ir) brave. Devland
  Devlen Devlyn

Dewei (Ch) virtuous

Dewey (E) morning dew. Dewie

Dewi (W) prized. Dewey

Dexter (L) dextrous, right-handed

Diarmuit see **Dermot**

Dick see **Richard**

Dickson (E) son of Richard. Dixon

Didier (F) desire. Desiderio

Digby (N) settlement by the dyke

Diggory (E) lost, strayed

Dimitri (Gk) belonging to Demeter. Demeter Demetre Demetrio Demetrius Dimitrios Dimitry Dimos

Dinesh (Sa) lord of the day

Dinsdale (W) born on Sunday

Dixon (E) son of Dick

Dolan (Ir) black-haired

Dominic (L) belonging to the Lord. Dom Dominick Nick

Donahue (Ir) warrior dressed in brown. Donaghue Donoghue Donohue

Donald (Ga) ruler of the world. Don Donal Donny Donyell

Donati (L) a gift. Donat Donatello Donatien

Donovan (Ga) dark warrior. Don

Donyell see **Donald**

Dooley (Ir) dark hero

Doran (C) stranger

Dorian (Gk) from the sea

Dory (F) golden-haired. Dorey

Dougal (Ga) dark stranger. Dougall

Douglas (Ga) from the dark water. Doug Dougy

Dov (H) bear

Doyle (Ir) assembly, swarthy

Draco (I) dragon

Dragan (Sl) dear one. Dragen

Drake (OE) dragon

Dray (E) cart. Draye

Drew (Ga) wise. See **Andrew**

Driscoll (Ir) interpreter. Driscol

Drury (F) dear one

Drydan (OE) from the dry valley

Duane (Ga) little dark one. Dwayne

Dudley (OE) from the meadow

Duff (Ga) dark

Duke (F) leader

Duncan (Ir) dark warrior

Dunley (E) from the meadow on the hill

Dunstan (E) from the dark hill. Dunstin

Duran (L) enduring, longlasting

Durant (L) enduring. Durand Durante

Durwin (E) dear friend. Durwyn

Dustin (E) valiant. Dustan Thurstan

Dwyer (Ir) dark, wisdom

Dylan (W) from the sea. Dillon Dylon

Eagle derived from the bird of the falcon family, strong

Eamon, **Eamonn** Irish forms of **Edmond**

Earl (E) man of high rank. Earle Errol

Eaton (OE) estate on the river

Eben (H) stone. Eban

Ebenezer (H) stone of help. Eben

Eden (H) delight

Edgar (E) rich, happy. Adair Edgaras Edgard Edgardo

Edison (OE) prosperity, wealth

Edmond (OE) rich protector. Eamon Eamonn Eddie Edmund Ned Ted

Edom (H) earthy. Esau

Edsel (OE) from the rich man's house

Edward (OE) rich guardian. Ed Eddie Edouard Eduard Eruera Ned Ted

Edwin (OE) happy friend. Ed Ned

Egan (Ga) fiery. Egon

Egbert (OE) bright sword. Bert Bertie

Egon (E) strong

Ehud (H) pleasant, sympathetic

Eilert (Sc) hardy, brave, strong

Einar (Sc) lone warrior
Eiros (W) bright
Elan (H) tree
Eland (E) from the island
Elden see **Alden**
Eldon (E) from the hill
Eldred (E) old. Aldred
Eldridge (E) from the alder tree ridge. Aldridge
Eleazar (H) God has helped
Elfed (W) autumn
Elgar (E) noble elf. Algar Alger Elger
✱**Eli** (H) height
Elijah (H) the Lord is God. Elias Eliot Elliot Elliott Ellis
Elisha (H) God is generous
Elkan (H) owned by God
Ellard (OE) noble, brave
Ellery (OE) elder tree
Elliot, **Ellis** English forms of **Elijah**
Ellison (E) son of Ellis or Elias
Elmer (I) protector
Elmo (Gk) amiable
Elmore (E) moor or river where elm trees grow
Elon (F) spirited
Elonzo (S) noble, famous. Alonzo

Elroy see **Leroy**
Elston (OE) estate of the old nobleman
Elton (OE) from the old farm. Eldon
Elvin see **Alvin**, **Elwin**
Elvio (S) blond
Elvis (N) all-knowing
Elwin (OE) friend of the elves. Elvin
Elwood (E) old wood
Emanuel (H) God is with us. Emmanuel Immanuel Manuel
Emerson (T) son of Emery
Emery (T) ruler. Emerick
Emil (T) industrious. Emile Emilio Emlyn
Emlyn Welsh form of **Emil**
Emmanuel see **Emanuel**
Emmet (Ir) surname derived from the German Emma
Emrys Welsh form of **Ambrose**
Emyr (W) honour
Enan (W) firm
Enlai (Ch) appreciation
Enoch (H) skilled
Enos (H) man
Enrico (I) Italian form of **Henry**

Enright (Ir) son of the attacker

Enzo (I) to win

Eoghan (Ir) born of yew. Eugene Evan Ewan Owen

Ephraim (H) meadows. Ephrem

Erasmus (Gk) loved, desired. Erasmo

Erastus (Gk) loving one

Eric (T) ruler. Erich Erik Rick

Ernan (Ir) iron

Ernest (T) vigorous. Earnest Ernst

Errol German form of **Earl**

Erskine (Ga) from the height of the cliff

Eruera Maori form of **Edward**

Erwin see **Irving**

Esau (H) hairy

Eskil (Sc) divinity. Esken

Esme (F) to love. Edme

Esmond (OE) graceful protector

Etera Maori form of **Ezra**

Ethan (H) perennial

Etienne French form of **Stephen**

Ettmore (I) steadfast

Euan see **Ewan**

Euclid (Gk) intelligent

Eugene (Gk) noble. Eugenio Gene

Eurig (W) golden

Eusebius (Gk) pious. Eusebio

Eustace (Gk) fruitful

Euston (Ir) heart

Evan Welsh form of **John**

Evander (Gk) good man

Everard (F) strong

Everest (OE) strong, brave

Everett (OE) strong. Everard

Everley (E) boar meadow. Eveleigh

Everton (E) boar village or town

Ewan (W) well-born. Euan Ewen Owen

Ewart (F) shepherd

Ewing (E) friend of the law

Ezekiel (H) may God strengthen. Ehekiera Zeke

Ezio (L) like an eagle

Ezra (H) helper. Etera

Fabian (L) bean grower.
Fabien

Fabrizio (I) craftsman. Brizio
Fabrice Fabricio

Fabron (F) little blacksmith.
Fabroni

Fadil (A) generous

Fagan (Ir) little fiery one.
Fagin

Fairfax (OE) fair-haired

Faisal (A) decisive. Faisel
Faizal Faysal

Falkner (E) trainer of
falcons. Falconer Falconner
Faulconer Faulkner

Fallon (Ir) leader

Fane (E) eager. Faine

Farley (OE) from the sheep
meadow. Fairley Fairlie

Farnell (E) hill of ferns.
Farnall Farnill

Farnham (E) field of ferns.
Farnam Farnum

Farold (E) robust traveller

Farook (A) truth. Farooq
Farouk Faruq

Farrell see **Fergal**

Faruq (A) honest. Farook
Farooq Farouk Faruqh

Faust (L) fortunate or lucky
one. Faustino Fausto
Faustus

Favian (L) man of
understanding

Felix (L) happy, lucky. Felice
Felicio Feliks

Felton (OE) from the estate
of the river. Felten

Fenlon (Ir) son of the fair
one

Fenn (E) marsh. Fen

Fenton (OE) from the
marshland farm

Fenwick (E) farm in the
marshland

Feodor Russian form of
Theodore

Ferdinand (T) bold
adventurer. Ferdy Fernand
Fernando

Fergal (Ga) man of strength.
Farrel Farrell Feargal
Ferrell

Fergus (Ga) chosen man.
Feargus

Ferguson (Ir) son of Fergus

Feroz (A) victorious. Feroze
  Firoz
Ferrand (F) grey-haired man
Ferrer (F) blacksmith. Ferrar
Ferris (Ga) man of the rock.
  Farris
Festus (L) steadfast
Fidel (L) faithful. Fidele
  Fidelio
Fielding (OE) from the field
Figaro (L) daring
Filbert (OE) brilliant. Fulbert
  Philbert
Filmer (OE) very famous.
  Filmore
Finbar (Ir) fair-haired
Findal (T) inventive
Fingal (Ga) white stranger
Finian (Ir) fair. Finnian
Finlay (Ga) fair-haired
  soldier. Findlay Finley
Finn (Ga) fair-haired
Finnegan (Ir) fair. Finegan
Fintan (Ir) little fair one
Fionn (Ir) fair
Fiorello (I) small flower
Firdos (A) paradise. Firdaus
Firmin (F) firm, steadfast.
  Fermin Firmino
Firth (E) of the forest
Fiske (Sc) fisherman. Fisk

Fitch (E) weasel. Fitche
Fitz (OE) son
Fitzgerald (F) son of Gerald
Fitzhugh (F) son of Hugh
Fitzjames (F) son of James
Fitzpatrick (F) son of Patrick
Fitzroy (F) son of the king
Flann (Ga) red-haired
Flavian (L) golden-haired.
  Flavien Flavio Flavius
Fleming (OE) Dutchman.
  Flemming
Fletcher (F) arrow maker
Flint (E) strong stone. Flynt
Florian (L) flowering. Florean
  Florien Floryan
Floyd English form of **Lloyd**
Flynn (Ga) son of the red-
  haired man. Flinn
Forbes (Ga) prosperous
Ford (OE) river crossing
Forrest (E) dweller of the
  forest
Fortescue (F) shield
Fortune (F) fortunate one.
  Fortunato Fortunio
Fox from the name of the
  animal
Francis (L) Frenchman.
  Francesco Franchot
  Francois Frank Frans Franz

Franklin (OE) free landowner. Frank

Fraser (OE) curly-haired. Frasier Frazer Frazier

Frederick (T) peaceful ruler. Fred Frederic Friedrich Fritz

Free (E) liberated. Freeway

Freeman (OE) born a free man

Frewin (E) free man

Fulton (OE) from the field

Fyfe (Ga) from Fife. Fife Fyffe

Gabriel (H) strong man of God. Gabby Gabe Gabel Gable

Gad (H) lucky. Gaddiel Gadiel

Gael (H) Gaelic-speaking people from Ireland and Scotland

Gage (F) pledge

Gaius (L) to rejoice. Caius Gaetano

Galahad (E) noble, selfless

Galbraith (Ir) Scottish man

Gale (F) gallant, brave. Gael Gaylor

Galen (Ga) intelligent. Gale

Gallagher (Ir) foreign helper

Galloway (Ir) foreigner

Galvin (Ir) the right one. Galvan Galven

Gamal (A) camel

Gamel (N) old. Gemmel

Gao (Ch) tall

Garcia (S) brave in battle

Gareth (W) gentle. Garry Garth Gary

Garfield (OE) field of war. Garry Gary

Garland (F) wreath. Garlan Garlen Garlyn

Garman (E) spear-carrier

Garner (T) warrior

Garnet (E) spear. Garnett

Garret Irish form of **Gerard**

Garrick (E) spear. Garek Gary

Garrison (E) from the place name Garriston

Garson (E) son of Gar

Garth see **Gareth**

Garvey (Ga) rough peace. Garvie

Garvin (E) friend with a spear. Garvan Garwin

Garwood (E) from the forest of fir trees

Gary see **Gareth**, **Garfield**, **Gerard**

Gaspar French form of **Jasper**

Gaston (F) from Gascony

Gavin (W) hawk of May. Gawain Gawn

Gaylord (F) high spirited, lively. Gallard Galor

Gene see **Eugene**

Geoffrey (T) peaceful. Geoff Jeff Jefferson Jeffrey

George (Gk) farmer. Geordie Hori

Geraint (Gk) old

Gerald (T) spear ruler. Gerry Jerry

Gerard (T) strong spear. Garret Garrett Gary Gerhard Gerhardt Gerry Jerry

German (L) from Germany. Germain

Gershom (H) stranger. Gersham Gershon Gerson

Gervais (T) spear servant. Gerry Gervase Jarvis

Gerwyn (W) fair love

Gethen (W) dark-skinned. Gethin

Gibson (E) son of Gilbert. Gibbons Gilson

Gideon (H) one-handed

Giffard (T) bold giver. Gifford

Gilbert (T) bright pledge. Bert Bertie Burt Gib Gil

Gilchrist (Ga) servant of Christ. Gil

Giles (Gk) young goat. Gilles

Gilford (E) near the ford

Gilmore (Ga) servant of Mary. Gil Gilmour

Gilroy (F) servant or son of a red-haired man

Girvan (Ir) rough one. Girvin

Gitano (S) gypsy

Gladstone (E) dweller near the rocks

Gladwin (E) happy, kind friend

Glanville (F) area of oak trees

Glen see **Glyn**

Glyn (W) from the valley. Glen Glenn

Goddard (T) pious and firm

Godfrey (T) God's peace

Godric (E) good ruler. Godrick Goodrich

Godwin (OE) friend of God

Golding (E) son of a golden one

Goliath (H) revealing

Gomer (E) good

Gomez (S) man

Gonzalo (S) wolf

Gopal (Sa) cow guardian

Gordon (OE) hill on the plains

Gough (W) red-haired

Gowan (N) golden. Gowall

Grady (Ga) noble, illustrious

Graham (T) from the grey home. Graeme Grahame

Granger (E) farmer. Grainger Grange

Grant (F) tall

Grantham (E) from the large meadow

Granville (F) from the big town

Gratian (L) thankful. Graciano Graziano

Grayson (OE) the bailiff's son. Gray

Gregory (Gk) watchful. Greg Gregg Gregor

Gresham (E) from the village near the pasture

Griffin (W) lord. Griffith

Griffith (W) powerful chief or warrior. Griffiths

Grover (OE) from the grove. Grove

Gunther (T) bold in war. Gunnar Gunner Gunter

Gurion (H) strength of a lion. Guryon

Gustave (Sc) staff of the Goths. Gus Gustaf Gustav Gustavus

Guthrie (Ga) from the windy place

Gutierre (S) power warrior

Guy (F) guide

Gwyn (W) white, fair. Guin Gwinn Gwynne Wyn Wynne

Gwynfor (W) fair lord

Habib (A) loved one

Hadar (H) grandeur

Haddon (OE) from the heath valley. Hadden

Hadi (A) leader

Hadley (OE) from the heath. Hadleigh

Hadrian see **Adrian**

Hadwin (E) a friend in war

Hafiz (A) protector

Hagen (Ir) home ruler. Hagan Haggan

Hai (Ch) from the lake or sea

Haig (OE) enclosure

Hakan (NA) fiery one

Hakaraia Maori form of **Zachariah**

Hakim (A) wise. Hakeem

Hakon (N) useful. Hacon

Hal see **Henry**

Halbert (E) great hero. Hal Halburt

Haldan (Sc) half Danish. Haldane Halden

Hale (OE) dweller in the remote valley

Haley (E) from the hay meadow. Haleigh

Halford (E) valley, ford

Hali (Gk) from the sea

Halifax (E) from a holy field

Halim (A) gentle man

Hallam (N) one who lives at the rocks

Halsey (OE) from Hal's island

Halstead (E) lord of the manor. Halsted

Halsten (Sc) rock. Halston

Halyard (Sc) one who defends the rock. Halvar Halvor

Ham (E) home

Hamal (A) lamb

Hamid (A) thankful or grateful one. Hamadi Hamidi

Hamilton (OE) from the proud estate

Hamish Scottish form of **James**

Hammond (E) chief protector

Hamo (T) home. Hamlet Hamnet Hamon

Hamon (Gk) faithful

Hamuera Maori form of **Samuel**

Hamza (A) powerful

Hani (A) delighted

Hanif (A) believer. Hanef

Hank see **Henry**

Hanley (OE) from the high meadow. Hanly

Hans German form of **John**

Hansel (Sc) God is gracious

Hanson (E) son of Hans

Hao (Ch) good
Harbin (F) little warrior
Harcourt (F) fortified dwelling
Harden (E) son of a brave man
Hardy (T) bold. Hardie
Hare Maori form of **Charles**
Hari (Sa) one who removes evil
Harish (Sa) lord. Haresh
Harkin (Ir) red. Harken
Harlan (E) from rocky land. Harland Harlen Harlin Harlyn
Harley (E) from the pasture where hares live. Arlea Arley Harleigh
Harold (OE) army leader. Harald Harry
Haroun (A) exalted
Harper (OE) harp player
Harris (OE) Harry's son. Harrison
Harry see **Harold**, **Henry**
Hartley (E) meadow with deer. Hartlee Hartleigh
Harvey (F) battle-worthy. Hervey
Harwin (E) brave friend. Hardwin Hardwyn Hartwin

Hasan (A) handsome. Hassan
Hasim (A) decisive. Haseem
Haslett (OE) from the hazel trees
Havelock (Sc) sea battle
Haven (OE) safe place
Hawk from the name of the bird, sharp
Hayden (OE) from the valley
Heath (E) heath
Heathcliffe (E) from a cliff near a heath. Heathcliffe
Heathcote (E) one from the home on the heath
Heaton (E) from the high town
Hector (Gk) steadfast
Heddwyn (W) blessed peace
Heman (H) faithful one
Hemi Maori form of **James**
Henare Maori form of **Henry**
Henderson (E) son of Henry
Hendy (E) polite, courteous
Henley (E) high meadow. Hanley
Henry (T) ruler of the estate. Enrico Hal Hank Harry Henare Hendrick Henri
Herbert (T) brilliant warrior. Bert Herb Herbie
Hercules (Gk) very strong

Herman (T) soldier. Armand Armin Harmon

Hermenegildo (S) one who makes a great sacrifice. Ermengilde Ermengildo

Hernando (S) brave traveller

Hershel (H) joyous. Herschel Heshel Hirsh

Hervey see **Harvey**

Hesperus (Gk) evening star. Hespero Hesperos

Hew see **Hugh**

Hiam (H) God's judgement

Hilary (L) cheerful. Ellery Hilaire Hilario Ilario

Hilton (OE) from the farm on the hill

Hiram (H) noble. Hi

Ho (Ch) goodness

Hoane, **Hoani** Maori forms of **John**

Hobson (E) son of Robert

Hodgson (E) son of Roger

Hoera Maori form of **Joel**

Hogan (Ga) youth

Hohepa Maori form of **Joseph**

Hohua Maori form of **Joshua**

Holbrook (E) from the brook or river in a valley

Holden (OE) from the valley

Holman (E) one who lives in the hollow

Holmes (N) from the river flat

Holt (OE) from the forest

Homer (Gk) pledge

Hona Maori form of **Jonah**

Hone Maori form of **John**

Horace (L) time keeper. Horatio Horatius

Hori Maori form of **George**

Horomona Maori form of **Soloman**

Horton (E) from the muddy place. Horten

Hosea (H) salvation

Houston (NA) one from the place of Hugh. Hewston Huston

Howard (T) guardian of the soul. Howie

Howell (W) eminent. Hywel

Hu (Ch) tiger

Hubert (T) bright mind. Bert Hobart Hubbard

Hudson (E) son of the hooded man

Hugh (T) heart, mind. Hew Hewett Huey Hugo Huw

Humphrey (T) peaceful. Humfrey Humphry

Hunter (E) hunter
Huntington (E) from the hunting estate
Huntley (E) hunter's meadow. Huntly
Huo (Ch) fire
Hura Maori form of **Judah**
Hurley (Ir) surname derived from O'Urthaile
Hussain (A) handsome young one. Hasan Hussein
Hutton (OE) from the farm on the ridge
Huxley (E) from the ash tree forest
Hyatt (OE) high gate
Hyde (E) plot of land
Hyman (H) life. Chaim Hyam Hymie
Hywel see **Howell**

Iago (S) he who supplants. Santiago
Iain, **Ian** Scottish forms of **John**

Ibrahim (A) father of many
Ichabod (H) the glory has gone
Idris (W) fiery lord
Ifor Welsh form of **Ivor**
Igasho (NA) wanderer
Ignatius (L) ardent. Iggy Ignace Ignacio Ignacius Inigo
Ihaka Maori form of **Isaac**
Imran (A) strong
Incencio (S) white one
Indra (Sa) raindrop
Ingemar (Sc) famous son
Inger (Sc) son's army
Ingram (T) heavenly raven
Ingvar (N) protector of Ing, the Norse god of peace and fertility
Inigo see **Ignatius**
Inir (W) honour
Innes (Ga) island in the river. Innis
Ira (H) watchful
Irvine (OE) friend of the sea. Ervn Erwin Irvin Irwin
Irving (E) from the sea. Ervin Erwin Irvin Irvine
Irwin (E) friend. Ervin Erwin Irwyn

GEM, MINERAL AND METAL NAMES

Boys	*Girls*
Carnelian	Amber
Cornelian	Amethyst
Flint	Crystal
Garnet	Diamond
Jet	Ebony
Onyx	Emerald
Slate	Garnet
Steel	Gemma
Topaz	Jade
	Jewel
	Opal
	Pearl
	Ruby
	Sapphire

Isaac (H) God may laugh.
Ihaka Ike Isaak Izaak

Isam (A) pledge

Ishmael (H) God hears

Isiah (H) God is generous.
Ihaia Isa

Isidore (Gk) a gift from the
Egyptian goddess Isis.
Esidor Isador Isidoro

Israel (H) may God prevail

Ivan Russian form of **John**

Ives (E) little archer

Ivor (Ga) archer. Ifor Yves

Ivory (Af) ivory

Jabez (H) sorrow

Jabir (A) consolation

Jack see **Jacob**, **John**

Jackson (OE) Jack's son

Jacob (H) supplanter.
Hamish Hemi Jack Jacky
Jacques Jaime Jake James
Jay Jim Jimmy Seamus
Seumus Shamus

Jael (H) ascend

Jagdish (Sa) world leader

Jake see **Jacob**

Jakeem (A) noble

Jalal (A) to be great

Jaleel (A) handsome

Jamal (A) handsome

James English form of **Jacob**

Jamieson (E) Son of Jamie.
Jameson Jamison

Jan see **John**

Janson (Sc) son of Jan.
Jansen Jantzen Janzen

Jared (H) rose

Jarvis see **Gervais**

Jason (Gk) healer. Jay

Jasper (P) treasure seeker.
Caspar Gaspar Kaspar

Jaspeth (H) beautiful

Jay (OE) blue jay

Jedidiah (H) friend of God.
Jed

Jefferson see **Geoffrey**

Jeffrey see **Geoffrey**

Jelani modern name,
derivation unknown

Jeremy (H) exalted by God.
Heremaia Jem Jemmy
Jeremiah Jerry

Jericho (A) city of the moon.
Jerico

Jermaine (F) German. Germain Jermain

Jerome (Gk) sacred name. Jerry

Jerry see **Gerald**, **Gerard**, **Jeremy**, **Jerome**

Jesse (H) God exists. Jess

Jesus Greek form of **Joshua**, God is salvation

Jet (L) from the colour black. Jett

Jethro (H) abundance

Jie (Ch) wonderful boy

Jim see **Jacob**

Jing (Ch) essence, pure

Joab (H) praise God

Joachim (H) may God exalt. Joaquin

Job (H) persecuted one

Jock see **John**

✱**Joel** (H) the Lord is God. Hoera

John (H) God is gracious. Evan Hans Hoane Hoani Hone Iain Ian Ivan Jack Jacky Jan Jock Johnny Jon Keshon Sean Shane Shaun Shawn Shawnel Zane

Johnson (E) son of John. Jonson Johnston

✱**Jonah** (H) dove. Hona Jonas

Jonathan (H) God has given a son. Jon Jonathon

Joram (H) the Lord is great

Jordan (H) flowing down

Joseph (H) God shall add. Hohepa Joe Joey Josef Jozef

Joshua (H) God is generous. Hohua Jesus Josh

Josiah (H) may God heal. Josh

Jotham (H) God is perfect

Judah (H) God leads. Hura Judd Jude

Julian (Gk) downy. Jules Julius

Julius (L) young, born in July. Giulio Jules Julian Julio

Jun (Ch) truth

Junior (E) young

Junius (L) born in June

Justin (L) fair. Guistino Justino Justinus Justo Justus Justyn Yestin

Kacey (E) man who speaks of peace. Kasey
Kadar (A) powerful. Kadir Kedar Qadir
Kadin (A) friend. Kadeen
Kaelan (Ir) strong soldier. Kalan Kalen Kalin
Kafeleb (Af) boy worth dying for
Kahanu (Ha) he breathes
Kahil (Gk) beautiful boy. Cahil Kahlil Kaleel
Kai (Ha) from the sea
Kaj (Gk) from the earth
Kala (As) black
Kale (Ha) man
Kalea (Ha) joy
Kalil (A) good friend. Kahlil Khalil
Kaliq (A) artistic one
Kalmin (Sc) man
Kamal (A) perfect one. Kamahl Kameel Kamil
Kanai (Ha) winner
Kane (C) radiant
Kang (Ch) healthy

Karam (A) charitable. Kareem Karim
Karif (A) boy born in autumn. Kareef
Karim (A) generous. Kareem
Kario see **Mario** (Mark)
Karl German form of **Charles**
Karma (Sa) star
Karmi (H) from my vineyard
Karney (Ir) winner. Carney Carny Karny
Karsten (Gk) blessed
Kasib (A) fertile one. Kaseeb
Kasimir (Sl) one who talks of peace
Kateb (A) writer
Kaul (A) trustworthy
Kay (W) joy. Kai
Keane (E) one with a sharp mind, bold one. Kean Keen Keene
Keanu (Ha) breeze across the mountains
Kearn (Ir) dark. Kern
Kearney (Ir) winner. Karney Kearney
Keaton (E) from the place where hawks fly. Keeton Keyton
Keefe (Ga) handsome
Keegan (Ga) fiery

Keelan (Ir) small one
Keeley (Ir) handsome boy. Kealey
Keenan (Ga) ancient
Kefir (H) lion club
Keir (C) dark-skinned
Keith (W) from the forest. Keth
Kele (NA) hawk (the bird)
Kell (N) one from the well or spring
Kelly (Ga) warrior
Kelsey (Sc) from the island
Kelton (E) from a town of ships
Kelvin (C) lover of ships
Kemp (E) fighter
Kempton (E) from a town of fighters
Ken see **Kenneth**
Kenan (H) one who strives to attain
Kendall (OE) from the valley of the river Kent
Kendrick (E) noble hero. Kendrik Kendryck
Kenelm (OE) brave warrior
Kenley (E) from the king's meadow. Kenleigh Kenly
Kennard (OE) hearty, strong
Kennedy (Ga) helmeted chief

Kenneth (Ga) handsome. Ken Kenny
Kent (C) bright
Kenton (OE) from the royal estate
Kenward (E) protector. Kenway
Kenway (E) brave one
Kenwyn (W) splendid leader
Kenyon (Ir) blonde boy
Keola (Ha) life
Keon (Ir) well-born. Kion
Kerel (Af) young man
Kermit (Ir) one without jealousy
Kerr (N) from the marsh. Carr
Kerry (Ga) dark-haired
Kerwin (Ir) little dark one. Kervin Kervyn Kerwen Kerwinn
Kes (E) falcon
Kesha modern name, derivation unknown
Keshon see **Sean**
Kester see **Christopher**
Kevin (Ir) handsome. Tevin
Khaldun (A) eternal. Khalid
Khalid (A) live forever, eternal
Khalif (A) successor, chief

Khalil (A) successor
Kieran (Ga) small and dark. Kieron
Kilian (Ir) warlike one. Keelan Killian Killin
Kim (OE) chief
Kimball (OE) war chief
Kingsley (OE) from the king's meadow
Kingston (OE) from the royal estate
Kinnard (Ir) from the tall hill
Kipp (E) a pointed hill
Kiran (Sa) ray of light
Kirby (Sc) from the church village
Kirk (Sc) from the church
Kishore (Sa) colt
Kit see **Christopher**
Kivi (Sc) dweller by a stone
Knox (OE) from the hills
Knut (N) knot. Knute
Kodiak (R) island
Koren (H) shining one
Kort (Sc) wise counsellor
Krishna (Sa) pleasurable, dark
Kumar (Sa) son
Kurt German form of **Conrad**
Kyle (Ga) from the strait
Kyne (E) royal one

Kyros (Gk) master

Laban (H) white
Lachlan (Ga) warlike
Lacy (F) lace. Lacey
Ladan (H) witness
Ladd (E) young man
Ladislav (Sl) great leader. Ladislas Ladislo Laszlo Vladislav
Lael (H) boy belonging to God
Lafayette (F) faithful
Laird (Ga) landowner
Lal (Sa) beloved
Lamar (T) famous throughout the land. Lamarr
Lambert (T) bright land. Bert
Lamech (H) powerful one
Lamond (Sc) lawman
Lance (T) of the land. Lancelot

Lancelot (F) one who guards the lance or spear. Launcelot

Landon (E) one from the grassy meadow. Landen Landin

Lane (OE) narrow country road. Layne

Lang (N) the tall one. Lange

Langdon (E) from the long hill. Langden

Langford (E) one from the long ford

Langley (E) one from the long meadow. Langleigh

Laramie (F) tears of love

Larkin (Ir) cruel

Laron (F) thief

Larry see **Laurence**

Lars Swedish form of **Laurence**

Larson (Sc) son of Lars

Lasairian (Ir) flame. Laserian

Latham (N) from the barn

Lathrop (E) from the farm with barns

Latif (A) gentle, kind. Lateef

Latimer (OE) interpreter

Laurence (L) bay tree. Larry Lars Laurens Laurent Laurie Lawrence

Lawson (E) son of Lawrence

Lawton (E) from the town on the hill. Laughton

Layne see **Lane**

Layton (E) herb garden. Leighton Leyton

Leander (Gk) like a lion

Leben (H) life

Lee (OE) from the meadow. Leigh

Leggett (F) messenger

Lei (Ch) thunder

Leibel (H) lion. Leib

Leif (Sc) beloved

Leighton (OE) from the meadow farm. Layton

Leland (E) meadow land. Layland Leyland

Lemuel (H) devoted to God

Lennon (Ir) cape, cloak

Lennox (Ga) elm trees

Leo (L) lion. see also **Leonard, Leopold**

Leon see **Lionel**

Leonard (T) bold as a lion. Lannard Len Lenny Leo

Leondra see **Leon**

Leopold (T) bold for the people. Leo

Leron (H) song

Leroy (F) the king. Elroy Leroi LeRoy Roy

Leslie (Ga) from the grey fort. Les Lesley

Lester (OE) from Leicester

Leverett (F) little rabbit. Leveritt Levert

Levi (H) pledged

Lewin (E) beloved friend

Lewis (T) famous warrior. Aloysius Lew Lou Louie Louis Ludovic Luigi Luis

Li (Ch) strength

Liam Irish form of **William**

Liang (Ch) good

Lin (Ch) forest

Lincoln (E) lake settlement

Lindell (E) from the valley of linden trees. Lindleigh Linley

Lindsay (OE) linden tree. Lindsey Linsay Linsey

Linford (E) from the ford of the linden trees. Lynford

Linton (E) from the town of linden trees. Lynton

Linus (Gk) flaxen-haired

Lionel (F) little lion. Leon Leondra Lyall

Liron (H) my song. Lyron

Lister (E) one who dyes cloth

Llewelyn (W) leader. Llewellyn Llywelyn

Lloyd (W) grey. Floyd Loyd

Locke (OE) from the forest. Lockwood

Logan (Ga) from the hollow

Loman (Ir) delicate one

Lon (Ir) brutal, hard one. Lonny

Lorcan (Ir) small, fierce one

Lorimer (L) harness maker

Lorne (OE) bereft

Louis French form of **Lewis**

Loukanos (Gk) one from Lucania. Lukianos

Lovell (F) dearly beloved. Lowe Lowel Lowell

Lowell (OE) little wolf. Loval Lovell Lowall

Lucan (Ir) derivative of Lucius

Lucas see **Lucius**

Lucian (L) shining. Lucien

Lucius (L) light. Luca Lucas Luck Lucky Luis Luke Ruka

Ludlow (E) from the leader's hill

Lugono (Af) sheep

Luis Spanish form of **Lucius**

Luister (Af) listener

Luke (L) one with light. Loucas Loukas Lucas Luce Lucian Lucien Lucius Luka Lukacs Lukas Ruka
Lundy (F) born on a Monday
Lunn (Ir) strong one. Lon Lonn
Luther (T) famous warrior. Lothaire
Lyall see **Lionel**, **Lyle**
Lyle (F) from the island. Lisle Lyall Lyell
Lyman (E) one from the meadow. Leyman
Lyndon (OE) linden tree. Lind Linden
Lynn (W) waterfall. Lin Linn Lyn
Lysander (Gk) liberator. Lisandro Sandy

Mabon (W) son
Mace (F) club (the weapon)
Mackenzie (Ga) son of the wise leader
Mackinley (Ir) wise leader. MacKinley
Macmahon (Ir) son of the bear. MacMahon
Macmurray (Ir) son of the mariner. MacMurray
Macnair (Ga) son of the heir
Maddox (W) fortunate, generous. Maddock Madoc Madog Madox
Madison (E) son of a soldier
Madoc (W) fortunate
Madron (L) noble
Mael (W) prince
Magee (Ir) son of Hugh. MacGee
Magnus (L) great
Magus (Gk) magician
Mahesh (Sa) great leader
Mahir (H) industrious
Mahmud (A) worthy of praise. Mahmood Mahmoud
Mahon (Ir) bear
Maimun (A) lucky one
Major (L) greater
Maka Maori form of **Mark**
Makarios (Gk) blessed. Macario Macrios Makar
Makram (A) noble

Malachi (H) my messenger.
  Mal Maraki
Malcolm (Ga) disciple of
  Columba. Colm Colum
Malik (A) master. Maliq
Malin (E) small warrior.
  Mallin
Mallory (F) soldier
Maloney (Ir) churchgoer.
  Malone Malony
Malvern (W) from the bare
  hill
Malvin see **Melvin**
Manal (A) one who achieves
Manar (A) one who inspires
Mandela from Nelson
  Mandela
Mansfield (E) from the field
Manfred (T) man of peace
Mani (Sa) jewel
Manley (E) from the man's
  meadow. Manleigh Manly
Manning (E) son, man
Mannix (Ir) small monk
Mano (Ha) shark
Mansa (Af) king
Mansel (E) from the
  clergyman's home. Mansell
Mansfield (E) from the field
  by the river

Mansur (A) victorious.
  Mansoor Mansour
Manu (M) bird, kite
Manuel see **Emanuel**
Manville (F) from the good
  town. Mandeville Manvill
Marc French form of **Mark**
Marcus see **Mark**
Mario (I) see **Mark**
Marion (F) defiant
Mark (L) warlike. Maka Marc
  Marcus Mario Marius
  Markus
Marley (E) from the
  meadow. Marleigh Marly
Marlon see **Merlin**
Marlow (E) hill near a lake.
  Marlo Marlowe
Marmaduke (Ir) son of
  Madoc. Duke
Marmion (F) small one
Marquis (E) nobleman
Marsh (E) from the marsh
  land
Marshall (OE) steward.
  Marshal
Martin (L) warlike. Marty
Marvin see **Mervyn**
Masio see **Thomas**
✱**Mason** (E) stone worker

NAMES OF AUTOMOBILES

Boys

Astin
Austin
Bentley
Benz
Chevy
Daimler
Edsel
Ford
Holden
Lincoln
Morris
Royce

Girls

Lada
Lancia
Lexus
Lotus
Mercedes
Morgan
Opel
Porsche

Mather (E) from the mighty army

Matiu Maori form of **Matthew**

Matok (H) sweet one

Matthew (H) gift of God. Mathew Matiu Matt Matteo Matthias Mattias Matty

Maurice (L) a Moor, dark-skinned. Baurice Morris

Maximilian (L) the greatest. Max Maxim

Maxwell (OE) from the well. Max

Maynard (T) strong, hardy

Mead (E) one from the meadow

Meallan (Ir) small pleasant one. Mellan

Meir (H) bright. Mayer Meyer Myer

Melvin (Ga) smooth-browed chief. Malvin Mel Melvyn

Mercer (F) merchant, shopkeeper

Meredith (W) protector of the sea

Merivale (E) blackbird

Merlin (E) falcon. Marlon

Merrick (W) dark one. Merryck

Merrill (E) son of Muriel. Merle Merrell Merryl

Merton (E) from the town by the lake

Mervyn (W) lover of the sea. Marvin

Micah (H) who is like God? Mika

Michael (H) who is like the Lord? Michail Michel Micky Mikaere Mike Mitch Mitchell

Michelangelo (I) Michael the angel

Mika Maori form of **Micah**

Mikaere Maori form of **Michael**

Miles (T) merciful. Milo

Miller (E) miller

Milo German form of **Miles**

Milson (E) son of Miles

Milton (OE) from the mill town. Millton

Ming (Ch) bright, clever

Minor (L) younger one. Mynor

Mitchell see **Michael**

Mohammed (A) praise.
Mohamad Mohamed
Mohammad
Mohan (Sa) bewitching
Monroe (F) from near the
Roe River in Ireland.
Monro Munro Munroe
Montague (F) from Mont
Aigu. Montagu Monty
Monte (L) mountain
Montel (E) mountain
Montgomery (L) mountain
hunter. Monty
Morcant (W) brilliant
Mordecai (H) follower of
Marduk
Morgan (W) from the sea
Morris see **Maurice**
Morrison (E) son of Maurice
Mortimer (F) still water.
Mort
Morton (OE) from the farm
on the moor
Moses (H) saved. Moss
Mosi (Af) first born
Moss see **Moses**
Muir (Ga) from the moor
Mungo (Ga) amiable
Munir (A) illuminating,
bright one. Muneer

Murdoch (Ga) sea man.
Murdock Murtagh
Murphy (Ga) sea warrior
Murray (Ga) sailor. Murry
Mustafa (A) chosen one.
Mustapha
Myron (Gk) fragrant oil

Nabil (A) noble one
Nadim (A) friend. Nadeem
Nadir (A) dear, precious one
Nahum (H) consoling. Naham
Nahumu
Naj (A) to save. Nagi Naji
Najib (A) smart one. Nagib
Najeeb
Naldo (S) one who gives
good advice
Namir (H) leopard
Nanda (Sa) joy
Napoleon (Gk) lion of the
new city
Narayan (Sa) son of man
Narcissus (Gk) daffodil.
Narcisse

Narenda (Sa) mighty one

Naresh (Sa) ruler

Nash (E) from the cliff. Nashe

Nasim (A) breeze. Naseem

Nasir (A) helpful, supportive one. Nassar Nasser

Natesh (Sa) destroyer. Natesa

Nathan (H) gift. Nat Nate

Nathaniel (H) God has given. Nat Nate Nathanael

Navarro (S) land. Navarre

Neal see **Neil**

Nectarios (Gk) saint

Ned see **Edmond**, **Edward**, **Edwin**

Neil Scottish form of **Nigel**

Nelson (OE) son of Neil

Nemesio (S) one who is just

Nemo (Gk) one from the glen or glade

Nero (L) stern

Nesbit (E) from the curve in the road or river. Nesbitt Nisbet Nisbett

Nestor (Gk) wise man

Nevada (S) snow

Neville (F) from the new town

Nevin (OE) nephew

Newell (E) one from the new hall. Newall

Newland (E) one from the new land

Newman (E) newcomer

Newton (E) one from the new town

Niall Irish form of **Nigel**

Nicholas (Gk) victory of the people. Claus Cole Colin Klaus Niccolo Nick Nickolas Nicky Nicol Nicolai Nicolas Nikita Nikolas Nikos

Nicodemus (Gk) conqueror. Nicodeme Nikodemos

Nicomedes (Gk) to ponder victory. Nikomedes

Nigel (Ir) champion. Neal Neale Neil Neill Niall

Niles (E) son of Neil

Nimrod (H) valiant hunter, rebel

Nino (S) young child

Nissan (H) sign, omen. Nisan

Nixon (E) son of Nicholas. Nickson

Noah (H) long-lived

Noam (H) delightful

Noble (L) noble one. Nobel

Noel (F) born on Christmas Day
Nolan (Ga) noble
Norbet (F) light from the north
Norman (T) man from the north. Norm
Norris (T) from the north
Northcliff (E) one from the north cliff. Northcliffe Northclyffe
Northrop (E) from the northern farm. Northrup
Norton (E) one from the northern town
Norville (E) one from the northern estate or town. Norval Norvel Norvil
Norvin (E) friend from the north. Norvyn Norwin
Norwood (E) one from the north wood
Numa (A) kindness
Nuncio (I) messenger. Nunzio
Nur (H) fire
Nuren (A) bright light
Nye see **Aneurin**

Oakes (E) one who lives by the oak trees
Oakley (E) one who lives by the oak tree meadow or clearing. Oakly
Obadiah (H) serving God. Oparia
Oban (L) citizen
Octavius (L) eighth child
Odell (N) wealthy one. Dell
Odin (N) ruler
Ogden (OE) from the oak valley. Ogdon
Ogilvie (Ga) high peak
Olaf (N) ancestral relics. Olav
Oliver (L) olive tree. Olivier Olly
Omar (A) first son
Ophir (H) faithful one
Oran (Ga) pale-skinned. Oren
Ordell (L) beginning
Oren (H) tree
Orestes (Gk) man from the mountains. Oreste
Orion (Gk) son of fire

Orlan (E) one from the sharp land

Orlando Italian form of **Roland**

Ormond (OE) protector

Oro (S) golden-haired

Orson (L) like a bear

Orton (E) from the town by the river

Orville (F) golden city

Osbert (E) divine one

Osborne (E) divine fighter. Osborn Osbourne Osburne

Oscar (OE) God's spear

Osgood (E) godly

Osmar (E) glorious, wonderful one

Osmond (OE) protected by God

Osten (L) esteemed one. Ostin

Oswald (OE) divine power

Oswin (E) divine friend. Oswinn Oswyn Oswynn

Otis (T) wealthy

Oved (H) worshipper, follower of God. Obed

Ovid (H) well-born one. Ewan Owain Owayne Owin

Owen see **Ewan**

Oxford (E) from the land of the oxen

Oz (H) power

Pablo Spanish form of **Paul**

Paddy Irish form of **Patrick**

Padgett (F) young attendant. Page

Padraig Irish form of **Patrick**

Page (F) young attendant. Paige

Paine (F) countryman. Payne

Pakelo (Ha) stone, solid. Peka

Palmer (OE) palm bearer

Panas (Gk) immortal one

Panos (Gk) rock

Paolo Italian form of **Paul**

Paoro Maori form of **Paul**

Paris (Gk) Trojan hero

Park (OE) from the park. Parke

Parker (OE) park keeper

Parkin (E) small Peter

Parnell see **Peter**

Parry (W) Harry's son

Parson (L) from the church

Pascal (I) born at Easter. Pascoe Pask

Patrick (L) nobleman. Paddy Padraig Pat Patrice

Patton (E) warrior. Patten

Paul (L) small. Pablo Paolo Paoro Pavel

Pavel Russian form of **Paul**

Pax (L) peace. Paz

Paxton (E) town of peace. Paxon Paxten

Payton (OE) settlement

Pedro Spanish form of **Peter**

Peer Norwegian form of **Peter**

Peleke (Ha) wise one

Pembroke (C) from the headland

Penley (E) from the pen or meadow. Penleigh

Penn (OE) enclosure

Penwyn (W) fair-haired one

Pepper from the name of the spice

Perben (Gk) stone

Percival (F) pierce the valley. Perceval Percy Perry

Percy (F) from Perci. See also **Percival**

Peregrine (L) traveller

Perry (OE) pear tree. See also **Percival**

Peter (Gk) stone. Parnell Pearce Pedro Peer Perrin Pete Petera Pierce Pierre Piers Pieter Pietro Pita

Petera Maori form of **Peter**

Phelan (Ir) wolf

Phelim (Ir) ever good

Phelps (E) son of Philip

Philbert see **Filbert**

Philemon (Gk) loving, kiss. Philo

Philip (Gk) lover of horses. Phil Phillip Piripi

Phineas (Af) negro. Phinehas

Phoenix (Gk) immortality

Piao (Ch) handsome one

Pierce see **Peter**

Pierre French form of **Peter**

Piers see **Peter**

Pierson (E) son of Peter. Pearson

Pilar (S) pillar

Pio (I) reverent

Piripi Maori form of **Philip**

Pita Maori form of **Peter**

Placido (S) placid, calm one

Pomeroy (F) one from the apple orchard

Porter (L) gatekeeper

Powell (W) alert
Prentice (F) apprentice.
  Prentis Prentiss
Prescott (E) one from the
  priest's cottage. Prescot
Presley (E) one from the
  priest's meadow. Presleigh
  Presly
Preston (OE) from the
  priest's farm
Prewitt (F) small brave one.
  Prewett Pruitt
Price (W) child with a loving
  father. Pryce
Primo (L) first son. Premo
Prince (L) first. Prinz Prinze
Prior (L) head of the
  monastery. Pryor
Probert (W) son of Robert
Proctor (L) an official.
  Procter
Prospero (I) fortunate,
  prosperous. Prosper
Purvis (F) provider. Purves

Qabim (A) ancient one
Qadir (A) talented one. Kadir
Qamar (A) moon
Qasim (A) provider. Kasim
Qayyim (A) right, generous
  one
Quennell (F) oak tree.
  Quennel Quinnell
Quentin (L) fifth. Quintin
Quigley (Ir) messy-haired
  one
Quillan (Ga) cub
Quimby (N) from a woman's
  house. Quemby Quenby
  Quinby
Quincy (F) from the fifth
  son's estate
Quinlan (Ga) strong
Quinn (Ga) wise
Quirin (E) magical
Quon (Ch) bright one. Quong
Qusay (A) distant

Rabi (A) breeze
Rachim (H) compassionate one. Racham Rahim
Rad (E) advisor
Radborne (E) from the red river or brook. Radbourn Radburn
Radcliffe (OE) red cliff
Radford (E) ford with reeds. Redford
Radley (E) from the red meadow. Radleigh
Radman (Sl) joy
Radnor (E) from the red beach
Radomil (Sl) peaceful one
Radwan (A) delight
Rafa (H) cure
Rafael see **Raphael**
Rafat (A) merciful one
Rafferty (Ir) prosperous one
Rafi (A) exalted one
Ragnar (Sc) wise warrior. Ragnor
Rahim (A) compassionate one. Rahman Rahmet

Raj (Sa) king, royal
Rajesh (Sa) king-like
Rajiv (Sa) striped one
Raleigh (E) one from the deer meadow. Ralweigh
Ralph (N) counsellor. Rafe Ralf Raoul Raul
Ralston (E) from Ralph's town
Ramsay (OE) from the ram's island. Ramsey
Ramsden (E) from the valley of rams
Rana (Sa) prince
Ranald see **Ronald**
Rand (E) fighter
Randal (OE) shield, wolf. Randall Randolph Randy
Randy see **Randal**
Ranger (E) protector of the forest. Rainger
Rangi (M) sky
Ranier (E) wise or strong counsellor
Raniera Maori form of **Robert**
Rankin (E) small shield
Ransley (E) one from the raven field
Raphael (H) God has healed. Rafael

Rapier (F) one with the strength of a sword

Rashard see **Richard**

Rasmus (Gk) beloved one

Rauf (A) compassionate one

Raul French form of **Ralph**

Ravid (H) wanderer

Raviv (H) rain

Rawiri Maori form of **David**

Ray (F) sovereign. See also **Raymond**

Rayhan (A) one loved by God

Raymond (T) mighty protector. Ray Raymund

Rayner (T) mighty army. Rainer Raynor

Read (E) red-haired one. Reed Reid Reide

Reading (E) son of the red-haired one. Reeding Reiding

Redman (E) rider

Reece see **Rhys**

Reed (OE) red-haired. Reade Reid

Rees see **Rhys**

Reeve (OE) steward

Regan (Ir) little king. Reagan Regan Regen

Regin (Sc) one with good judgement

Reginald (E) wise counsellor. Reg Reginalt Reginauld

Regis (F) leader

Reilly (Ir) descendant of the valiant one. Riley

Remington (E) from the raven farm

Remus (L) fast-moving

Remy (F) from the French town of Reims. Remi Remie Remmy

Renaud (F) powerful one

Rene (F) reborn

Renfred (E) good peace

Renfrew (W) from a calm river

Renny (Ir) small, strong one

Reuben (H) renewer. Ruben

Revere (L) respect

Rewi Maori form of **David**

Rex (L) king

Reynard (F) fox. Raynard Reinhard

Reynold (OE) powerful. Reg Reggy Reginald

Rhett (E) fiery one

Rhodri (W) ruler

Rhun (W) grand one

Rhys (W) impetuous. Reece Rees Rhett

Richard (T) firm ruler. Dick
Dicky Rashard Ricardo
Rich Richie Rick Ricky

Richmond (F) protector.
Richman

Rida (A) satisfied one

Rider (E) horseman. Ryder

Ridge (E) from the ridge

Ridley (E) from the red
meadow. Riddley Ridleigh
Ridly

Rigby (E) from the ruler's
valley

Riley (Ga) valiant. Reilly

Ringo (E) bell ringer

Rio (S) river

Riordan (Ir) poet. Rearden
Reardon

Ripley (E) from the shouter's
meadow. Ripleigh Riply

Rishon (H) first

River modern usage, a large
creek

Roark (Ir) mighty one. Rork
Rourke

Robert (T) bright fame.
Bob Bobby Rab Raniera
Rapata Rob Robin Rupert
Ruprecht

Robertson (E) son of Robert

Robin see **Robert**

Robinson (E) son of Robert.
Robeson Robson

Rocco (I) Italian form of
Roch

Roch (F) rest

Rochester (E) from the stone
fort. Chester Chet

Rockwell (E) from the well
near the rocks

Rocky modern usage, full of
rocks. Rock

Roderick (T) famous ruler.
Rod Roddy Roderic Rory

Rodger see **Roger**

Rodney (E) from the island
clearing. Rod Roddy

Roe (E) deer

Rogan (Ir) red-haired one

Rogelio (S) famous warrior

Roger (T) famous warrior.
Rodger

Rohan see **Rowan**

Roland (T) from the famous
land. Orlando Rolland Rollo
Roly Rowland

Rolf (T) famous wolf. Rollo
Rolph Rudolf Rudolph
Rudy

Roman (L) from Rome

Romeo (I) one who visits
Rome

Romney (W) one from the
winding river
Ronald (N) powerful. Ranald
Ron
Ronan (Ga) seal
Ronel (H) God's song
Roni (H) joyful, happy one
Ronson (E) son of Ronald
Roper (E) one who makes
rope
Rory (Ga) red
Roscoe (OE) from the place
name
Ross (Ga) from the headland
Rousse (F) red-haired one
Rove (E) wanderer. Rover
Rowan (Ga) red. Rohan
Rowland see **Roland**
Roy (Ga) red
Royal (F) royal one
Royce (OE) son of the king
Royd (Sc) one from the
forest
Royden (E) from the hill
growing rye. Roydon
Rozen (H) leader
Rudd (OE) ruddy complexion
Rudolph see **Rolf**
Rudyard (OE) from the red
enclosure
Ruford (E) from the red ford

Rufus (L) red-haired
Ruka Maori form of **Luke**
Rupert German form of
Robert
Rurik (Sc) king. Rorek Ruric
Rush (F) red
Ruskin (F) red-haired one
Russell (F) red-haired. Russ
Rusty
Rutherford (E) from the
cattle ford
Rutley (E) from the red field
Ryan (Ga) small king
Ryland (E) from the field of
rye. Ryeland

Saad (H) assistance
Sabir (A) patient one. Sabeer
Sabre (F) sword. Saber
Sacha Russian form of
Alexander
Sachiel (H) angel of water
Saddam (A) hard
Sadler (E) saddle maker.
Saddler

Safa (A) pure one
Sagar (Sa) ocean
Sage from the name of the plant
Sahen (Sa) falcon
Sahil (Sa) leader, guide
Said (A) cheerful one. Saeed Sayeed Sayid
Sailor (NA) sailor
Sajan (Sa) beloved one
Sakaria (Sc) God will remember. Sakari Sakarios Sakia
Saladin (A) virtuous. Saleh Salih
Salam (A) lamb
Salim (A) tranquil. Saleem Salem
Salman (A) high
Salvatore (I) saviour. Sal Salvador Salvator Salvidor
Sam see **Samson**, **Samuel**
Samal (H) symbol
Sameer (A) little breeze
Sami (H) exalted one
Samir (A) evening entertainer
Samson (H) child of the sun god. Sam Sampson
Samuel (H) in the name of God. Hamuera Sam

Sanborn (OE) sandy brook
Sancho (S) holy
Sandeep (Sa) enlightened
Sanders (E) defender. Sanderson Saunders Saunderson
Sandford (E) sandy crossing. Sanford
Sandy see **Alexander**
Sanjay (Sa) conscience
Sanjiv (Sa) revive. Sanjeev
Santiago (S) saint
Santo (I) holy one. Santos Sanzio
Sargent (F) officer. Sergeant Sergent
Saul (H) asked for
Saville (F) town of willows. Savil Savill
Sawyer (E) woodsman. Sayer
Saxon (OE) swordsman
Sayed (A) lord and master. Sayid
Sayer (T) victory for the people. Saer
Scanlon (Ir) scandal. Scanlan Scanlen
Scipio (L) staff. Scipion Scipione

113

NAMES OF FAMOUS NEW ZEALAND SPORTSPEOPLE

Boys

Bevan Docherty, triathlete
Chris Cairns, cricketer
Daniel Carter, rugby player
Danyon Loader, swimmer
David Tua, boxer
Dean Barker, sailor
Sir Edmund Hillary, climber
Hamish Carter, triathlete
John Walker, athlete
Jonah Lomu, rugby player
Nathan Astle, cricketer
Maz Quinn, surfer
Michael Campbell, golfer
Peter Snell, athlete
Possum Bourne, motorsport
Sir Richard Hadlee, cricketer
Sean Fitzpatrick, rugby player
Stephen Flemming, cricketer
Tana Umaga, rugby player
Zinzan Brooke, rugby player

Girls

Adine Wilson, netball player
Allison Roe, athlete
Anna Rowberry, netball player
Annalise Coberger, skiier
Barbara Kendall, sailor
Beatrice Faumuina, athlete
Bernice Mene, netball player
Caroline Evers-Swindell, rower
Emily Drumm, cricketer
Erin Baker, athlete
Georgina Evers-Swindell, rower
Heidee Tiffen, cricketer
Helen Clark, hockey player
Irene Van Dyk, netball player
Kamila Wihongi, rugby player
Mandy Smith, hockey player
Nicki Jenkins, gymnast
Sandra Edge, netball player
Sarah Ulmer, cyclist
Susan Devoy, squash player

Scott (OE) from Scotland. Scot

Scout modern usage, person sent out to spy

Scully (Ir) town crier

Seafra (Ir) with the peace of God. Seafraid Seathra

Seamus Irish form of **James**

Sean Irish form of **John**

Searle (T) warrior. Serle

Seaton (E) seaside town. Seton

Sebastian (L) venerable. Sebastien

Sedgwick (E) from the place of swords. Sedgewick

Segel (H) treasure

Seger (E) one who fights at sea. Seager Seeger

Segev (H) majestic

Seif (A) sword of religion

Selah (H) song

Selby (OE) from the manor farm

Seldon (OE) from the valley of the willows. Selden

Selig (T) blessed. Zelig

Selwyn (OE) friend at the manor house. Wyn

Senior (F) older

Sennett (F) venerable one. Sennet

Septimus (L) seventh

Seraphim (Gk) intense heat. Serafin Serafino

Serge (L) servant. Sergei Sergio

Seth (H) substitute

Seumus Irish form of **James**

Seven (S) Severe. Severin Severiano

Seward (OE) defender

Sexton (E) church official

Sextus (L) sixth

Seymour (F) from St Maur

Shad (H) short for Shadrach

Shakir (A) grateful one. Shakur

Shamus Irish form of **James**

Shandy (E) lively

Shane, Shaun Irish form of **John**

Shannon (Ir) old and wise

Shaquille (A) handsome

Sharif (A) honest. Shareef

Shaw (OE) from the grove

Shawn Irish form of **John**

Shawnel modern version of **Shawn**. Shawnell Shawnelle

Shay (Ir) stately. Shamus
 Shea
Shea (Ga) from the fairy fort
Sheehan (Ga) peaceful
Shelby (E) a willow grove
Sheldon (OE) hill ledge.
 Shelton
Shelley (E) from the meadow
 near the hill. Shelly
Shem (H) famous
Shepard (OE) shepherd.
 Shepherd Sheppard
Sheridan (Ga) wild
Sherlock (OE) fair-haired
Sherman (OE) shearer
Sherwood (OE) from the
 bright forest
Shiloh (H) he who is to be
 sent
Shimon (H) amazed
Sidney (F) from St Denis. Sid
 Sydney
Siegfried (T) peace after
 victory. Sigfrid Sigfried
Sigmund (T) victorious
 protector. Siggy
Silas (L) from the forest.
 Silvan Sylvan
Silvanus (L) one who dwells
 in the woods. Silas Silvain
 Silvano

Silvester see **Sylvester**
Simba (Af) lion
Simeon (H) one who listens.
 Simon
Simon Greek form of **Simeon**
Sinclair (F) shining light
Skeeter (E) swift. Skeat
 Skeet
Skip (E) ship's captain.
 Skipper Skippy
Sky see **Skylar**
Skylar from the Isle of Skye
 (Scotland)
Slater (E) one who lays slate
 on roofs
Sloan (Ga) warrior. Sloane
Smil (Sl) beloved
Smith (E) blacksmith.
 Schmidt Smyth Smythe
Smokey colour of smoke
Sol (L) the sun
Soloman (H) little man of
 peace. Horomona Shalom
Somerset (E) summer place.
 Somerby Sommerset
 Summerset
Sonny (E) dear one
Soren (Sc) strict, stern
Spencer (F) dispenser.
 Spence Spenser
Spike (E) long nail

Spiro (Gk) breath of the gods
Stacy (L) dependable. Stacey
Stafford (OE) landing place
Stamford (E) stony food.
  Stanford
Stanislas (Sl) camp glory.
  Stanislaus
Stanley (OE) from the rocky
  meadow. Stan
Steadman (E) one who owns
  a farm. Stedman
Stephen (Gk) crowned.
  Etienne Stefaan Stefan
  Stephan Stevan Steve
  Steven
Sterling (OE) honest. Stirling
Sterne (E) stern, austere.
  Stearne
Steve, **Steven** see **Stephen**
Stewart see **Stuart**
Stig (Sc) wanderer
Stirling see **Sterling**
Stoddard (OE) horse, herd
Storm storm, atmospheric
  disturbance
Stratford (OE) street across
  the ford
Stuart (OE) steward.
  Stewart
Sultan (A) prince
Suman (Sa) happy and wise

Sumner (L) summoner
Sun (Ch) descending
Sundar (Sa) good-looking
Sutherland (Sc) from the
  southern field
Sutton (OE) from the
  southern town
Sven (Sc) youth. Swen
Swaine (Sc) herdsman,
  servant
Sweeney (Ir) little hero
Sydney see **Sidney**
Sylvester (L) woody.
  Silvester

Tab (T) drummer
Taber (Ir) spring, well
Tad (Ir) philospher. Tadd
  Taddeo Tadeo
Taggart (Ir) son of the priest
Talbot (OE) wood cutter
Talib (A) seeker of truth
Taliesin (W) radiant brow
Talmai (H) mound

Talman (H) injured one.
  Talmon
Talon sharp claw
Tamati Maori form of
  Thomas
Tamson (Sc) son of Thomas.
  Tamsen
Tanguy (F) warrior
Tangwyn (W) peace
Tanner (E) person who tans
  leather hides. Tannon
Tannon see **Tanner**
Tao (Ch) peach
Tate (OE) cheerful
Taylor (OE) tailor. Tailor
Teague (Ir) poet. Teagan
  Tegan
Ted see **Edward**, **Theodore**
Telfor (E) surname, to cut
  iron
Templar (F) knight
Temple (OE) dweller near
  the temple
Templeton (E) village near
  the temple
Tennessee (NA) warrior
Tennyson (E) son of Dennis.
  Dennison Tennison
Terence (L) smooth. Terrence
  Terry
Terrant (W) thunder

Terrill (T) follower of Thor
Terry see **Terence**
Tevin see **Kevin**
Thaddeus (Gk) courageous.
  Thad
Thane (OE) military
  attendant
Thanos (Gk) noble
Theodore (Gk) gift of God.
  Feodor Ted Teddy Theo
Theron (Gk) hunter. Theran
  Theren
★**Thomas** (H) twin. Masio
  Tamati Thom Tom <u>Tomas</u>
  Tommy
Thornton (OE) from the
  thorny place
Thorpe (OE) from the village.
  Thorp
Thurstan (Sc) Thor's stone.
  Thurston
Tiare Maori form of **Charles**
Tiberius (L) from the River
  Tiber. Tibor
Tien (Ch) heaven
★(**Tiernan**) (Ir) little lord.
  Tierney
Timon (Gk) reward
Timothy (Gk) honouring God.
  Tim Timoti

119

Timoti Maori form of **Timothy**

Tito (Gk) to honour

Titus (L) of the giants. Tito Titos

Tobias (H) God is good. Toby Topia

Todd (L) fox. Toddy

Tom see **Thomas**

Tomkin (E) little Tom

Tonio, Tony see **Anthony**

Topia Maori form of **Tobias**

Tor (Ir) rock

Toussaint (F) all of the saints

Tovi (H) good

Trace modern name, follow the trail

Tracy (Gk) to manage. Tracey

Travers (F) crossroads. Travis

Tremaine (OE) from the place name, stone village

Trent (L) torrent

Trevor (Ga) discreet

Trey (L) three

Tristram (C) noisy. Tristan Tristrum

Troy (F) curly-haired

Truitt (E) small, honest one. Truett

Truman (OE) faithful

Tucker (E) one who works with cloth

Tug (Sc) pull, tug

Tully (Ir) the mighty people

Turner (E) woodworker

Tye see **Tyrone**

Tyler (OE) tile maker. Tiler

Tynan (Ir) dark one. Tinan

Tyrone (Gk) sovereign. Tye

Tyson (F) firebrand

Uccello (I) bird

Udell (E) from the valley of the yew trees. Udale Udall

Udo (Af) peace

Uhura (Af) freedom

Ulick see **Ulysses**

Ulmer (E) famous wolf

Ulric (OE) wolf ruler. Alaric Alric Rick Ulrich

Ulysses (L) angry. Ulick

Umar (A) flourishing. Omar

Unwin (E) enemy

Upton (E) from the upper farm
Urban (L) from the town
Uriah (H) God is light
Uriel (H) light. Ure Uri Urie Yuri
Ursel (L) bear. Ursell Urshell
Uziel (H) strength

Vaallis (F) man from Wales
Vachel (F) one who raises cows
Vail (OE) from the valley. Vale
Valdemar (F) strong. Val Valek Valencio Valentin Valentino Valentyn
Valentine (L) strong, healthy. Val Valentijn Valentin Valentino
Valerian (L) strong. Valerio Valery
Vamana (Sa) deserving of praise

Van (T) of noble descent. Vann
Vance (T) Van's son
Vangelis (Gk) evangelist
Varden (F) from the green hills. Vardon Verdin
Varian (L) changeable
Vaughan (W) small. Vaughn
Vaux (F) from the valley
Venn (E) from the marsh land or fenn. Vane
Verdi (L) green. Verdo
Vere (L) faithful
Verlin (L) spring-like
Vernon (L) flourishing. Vern Verne
Verrell (F) honest. Verill Verrall Verrill
Victor (L) conqueror. Vic Vick Vittorio
Vijay (Sa) victory
Vikesh (Sa) moon
Vikram (Sa) heroic
Vincent (L) conquering. Vince Vinnie
Vinson (E) son of Vincent
Virgil (L) staff bearer. Vergil
Vishnu (Sa) protector
Vitale (L) vitality. Vidal Vital Vitali Vito
Vito (L) life. Vitus

Vivian (L) alive
Vladimir (Sl) powerful prince
Vladislav (Sl) great leader.
  Ladislav Vlad

Wade (OE) wanderer
Waite (E) watchman, guard
Walby (E) from the farm
  with the old wall
Walcott (E) cottage near the
  embankment
Walden (E) from the valley in
  the forest. Waldon
Walford (E) from the ford
  across the stream
Walker (E) to tread
Wallace (OE) Welshman.
  Wallis Wally Walsh
Wally see **Wallace,Walter**
Walter (T) ruler of the
  people. Wally Walt
Wang (Ch) regal
Ward (OE) guardian
Wardell (E) from near the
  River Wear. Wardale

Warley (E) from the cattle
  pasture
Warmund (E) protector.
  Warmond
Warner (T) man of the
  people
Warren (T) defender
Warton (E) lookout point
Warwick (E) from the place
  at the weir. Warrick
Wasim (A) handsome.
  Waseem
Watkin (E) son of Walter.
  Watkins Watson
Waverley (E) from the place
  of aspen trees. Waverly
Wayland (OE) from the place
  near the road
Wayne (OE) wagon maker
Webb (E) weaver. Webber
  Weber Webster
Welby (E) from the farm by
  the spring
Weldon (E) from the hill with
  a spring
Wen (Ch) cultured
Wenceslas (Sl) glory.
  Wenceslaus
Wendell (T) traveller
Wentworth (E) winter
  estate

Wenzel (Sl) to know
Werahiko Maori form of
  Francis
Wesley (OE) from the
  western meadow. Wes
Weston (E) from the town in
  the west
Wheeler (E) wheel maker
Whib (A) generous one
Whitby (E) from the white
  town
Whitcombe (E) from the
  wide valley. Whitcomb
Whitfield (E) from the white
  field
Whitford (E) from the white
  ford
Whitley (E) from the white
  meadow
Whitmore (E) from the
  white moor
Whitney (E) from the white
  island. Whitny Witney
Whittaker (E) from the
  white field. Whitaker
Wickham (E) from the home
  in the meadow. Wykeham
Wilbur (T) resolute
Wilfred (T) resolute,
  peaceful. Wilf Willy

Willard (T) resolute, brave.
  Will Willy
William (T) resolute
  protector. Bill Billy Liam
  Will Willem Willy Wiremu
Wilson (OE) son of William
Wilton (E) from the farm
  with a well
Wing (Ch) glory
Winslow (E) from the
  friend's hill
Winston (OE) from the
  friendly town. Win Winnie
  Winton
Winter (E) born in the
  winter months
Wiremu Maori form of
  William
Wolf from the name of the
  animal
Woodley (E) from the
  meadow or forest
Woodrow (OE) hedge in the
  wood. Woody
Wray (Sc) dweller near the
  corner
Wren (E) small bird
Wyatt (F) guide
Wylie (OE) enchanter

Wyndham (OE) from the village with the winding path
Wynn (W) fair
Wynton (W) from the white place. Winton

Xanthus (Gk) golden-haired
Xavier (A) bright
Xenophon (Gk) strange voice
Xenos (Gk) stranger
Xerxes (P) ruler
Xylon (Gk) forest dweller. Zylon

Yael (H) mountain goat
Yakim (H) God will establish
Yakir (H) beloved

Yale (OE) from the corner of the land
Yang (Ch) bright
Yardley (E) from the meadow
Yasin (A) prophet
Yasir (A) wealthy. Yasar Yaseer Yasser
Yates (OE) from the gates
Yehudi (H) praise the Lord
Yin (Ch) silver
York (OE) estate of the boar. Yorick
Yu (Ch) jade
Yuan (Ch) original
Yule (E) born at Christmas. Yul Yules
Yves French form of **Ivor**

Zabdi (H) gift. Zavdi
Zaccheus (H) innocent one. Zacceus
Zachariah see **Zachary**
Zachary (H) God has remembered. Hakaraia Zachariah Zacharias Zack

Zadok (H) righteous, just.
  Zadoc Zaydok
Zafar (A) victorious,
  triumphant. Zafeer Zafir
Zahir (A) shining one. Zaheer
Zakariyya (A) prophet
Zake (A) pure, chaste one
Zaki (A) pure one. Zakia
  Zakkai
Zale (Gk) strength from the
  sea
Zamir (H) songbird
Zane see **John**
Zared (H) ambush
Zebedee (H) God has
  bestowed
Zebediah (H) gift from God.
  Zeb Zebadiah Zebedee
  Zedidiah
Zebulun (H) exalt. Zeb
Zedekiah (H) righteousness
  of God. Zed
Zeke see **Ezekiel**
Zelig see **Selig**
Zelotes (Gk) fervent,
  passionate one
Zenas (Gk) living
Zeno (Gk) cart. Zenas Zenon
  Zenus
Zephaniah (H) God has
  protected. Tepania

Zephyr (Gk) gentle wind
Zev (H) wolf
Zia (A) enlightened one
Zion (H) excellent sign. Sion
  Tzion
Ziskind (H) sweet child
Ziv (H) life. Ziven
Zoran (Sl) dawn
Zorba (Gk) live
Zorro (Sl) golden dawn. Zoro
Zubin (H) to exalt
Zuriel (H) God is my way

Your child and the stars

Aries 22 March to 20 April

Colour red; **Metal** copper; **Stone** diamond; **Character** pioneering, adventuring spirit, enterprising, courageous, direct in approach, highly energetic, freedom loving, unsubtle, impulsive, impatient, generous

Taurus 21 April to 21 May

Colours pink, pale blue; **Metal** copper; **Stone** sapphire; **Character** practical, reliable, patient, businesslike, enduring, persistent, solid, determined, affectionate, trustworthy, stubborn

Gemini 22 May to 22 June

Colours all, especially yellow; **Metal** mercury; **Stone** agate; **Character** adaptable, versatile, intellectual, witty, logical, spontaneous, lively, talkative, changeable, restless, young looking

Cancer 23 June to 23 July

Colours smokey greys, green; **Metal** silver; **Stone** pearl; **Character** kind, sensitive, sympathetic, powerful imagination, cautious, patriotic, tenacious, shrewd, thrifty, excellent homemaker

Leo 24 July to 23 August

Colours golden yellow, orange; **Metal** gold; **Stone** ruby; **Character** magnanimous, generous, creative, enthusiastic, good organiser, broad-minded, expressive, of fixed opinions

Virgo 24 August to 23 September

Colours navy blue, dark greys, browns; **Metal** mercury; **Stone** sardonyx; **Character** discriminating, analytical, tidy, conventional, hard-working, meticulous, modest

Libra 24 September to 23 October

Colours pale blue, pink; **Metal** copper; **Stone** sapphire; **Character** charming, harmonious, likes pleasant living conditions, easygoing, romantic, diplomatic, idealistic, refined

Scorpio 24 October to 22 November

Colours dark red, maroon; **Metal** iron; **Stone** opal; **Character** powerful feelings and emotions, a sense of purpose, highly imaginative, discerning, subtle, persistent, determined, stubborn

Sagittarius 23 November to 22 December

Colours purple, dark royal blue; **Metal** tin; **Stone** topaz;
Character jovial, optimistic, versatile, open-minded, adaptable,
freedom loving, sincere, frank, dependable, scrupulous

Capricorn 23 December to 19 January

Colours black, dark grey, very dark green, brown; **Metal** lead;
Stone turquoise; **Character** reliable, determined, ambitious,
careful, provident, a sense of humour, a sense of discipline,
patient, persevering

Aquarius 20 January to 19 February

Colour electric blue; **Metal** uranium; **Stone** amethyst; **Character**
humanitarian, independent, friendly, willing, progressive outlook,
original, inventive, a reforming spirit, faithful, loyal, idealistic

Pisces 20 February to 21 March

Colour soft sea-green; **Metal** tin; **Stone** moonstone, bloodstone;
Character humble, compassionate, sympathetic, emotional,
unworldly, sensitive, adaptable, impressionable, kind, intuitive,
receptive